Gatehouse to Hell

THE AZRIELI SERIES OF HOLOCAUST SURVIVOR MEMOIRS: PREVIOUSLY PUBLISHED TITLES

ENGLISH TITLES

Album of My Life by Ann Szedlecki

Bits and Pieces by Henia Reinhartz

A Drastic Turn of Destiny by Fred Mann

E/96: Fate Undecided by Paul-Henri Rips

Fleeing from the Hunter by Marian Domanski

From Generation to Generation by Agnes Tomasov

Getting Out Alive by Tommy Dick

Knocking on Every Door by Anka Voticky

Little Girl Lost by Betty Rich

Memories from the Abyss by William Tannenzapf/ *But I Had a Happy Childhood* by Renate Krakauer

The Shadows Behind Me by Willie Sterner

Spring's End by John Freund

Tenuous Threads by Judy Abrams/ *One of the Lucky Ones* by Eva Felsenburg Marx

Under the Yellow and Red Stars by Alex Levin

The Violin by Rachel Shtibel/ *A Child's Testimony* by Adam Shtibel

TITRES FRANÇAIS

L'Album de ma vie par Anne Szedlecki

Cachée par Marguerite Elias Quddus

Étoile jaune, étoile rouge par Alex Levin

La fin du printemps par John Freund

Fragments de ma vie par Henia Reinhartz

Matricule E/96 par Paul-Henri Rips

Objectif : survivre par Tommy Dick

Souvenirs de l'abîme par William Tannenzapf/ *Le Bonheur de l'innocence* par Renate Krakauer

Le violon par Rachel Shtibel/ *Témoignage d'un enfant* par Adam Shtibel

Gatehouse to Hell

Felix Opatowski

THE AZRIELI FOUNDATION
www.azrielifoundation.org

Cover and book design by Mark Goldstein
Endpaper maps by Martin Gilbert
Map on bottom of page xxiii by François Blanc
Map on top of page xxiii courtesy of the US Holocaust Memorial Museum
Map on page xxii courtesy of US Holocaust Memorial Museum and modified,
    with permission, by Keaton Taylor

LIBRARY AND ARCHIVES CANADA CATALOGUING IN PUBLICATION

Opatowski, Felix, 1924–
        Gatehouse to hell/ Felix Opatowski.

(The Azrieli series of Holocaust survivor memoirs. Series IV)
Includes bibliographical references and index.
ISBN 978-1-897470-26-8

1. Opatowski, Felix, 1924– 2. Holocaust, Jewish (1939–1945) – Poland – Personal narratives. 3. Holocaust survivors – Canada – Biography. 4. Polish Canadians – Biography. I. Azrieli Foundation. II. Title. III. Series: Azrieli series of Holocaust survivor memoirs. Series IV.

DS134.72.O63A3 2012   940.53'18092   C2011-908476-7

PRINTED IN CANADA

The Azrieli Series of Holocaust Survivor Memoirs

Contents

Series Preface   ix
About the Glossary   xi
Introduction *by Marlene Kadar*   xiii

Maps   xxii–xxiii

Prologue   1
My Childhood in Lodz   3
The War Begins   13
Weisser Adler   25
Auschwitz   37
The Neutral Zone   61
Uprising   85
Leaving Auschwitz   99
Liberation   117
Epilogue   133
"The Song of the Partisans"   143

Glossary   145
Photographs   167
Index   179

Series Preface:
In their own words...

In telling these stories, the writers have liberated themselves. For so many years we did not speak about it, even when we became free people living in a free society. Now, when at last we are writing about what happened to us in this dark period of history, knowing that our stories will be read and live on, it is possible for us to feel truly free. These unique historical documents put a face on what was lost, and allow readers to grasp the enormity of what happened to six million Jews – one story at a time.

David J. Azrieli, C.M., C.Q., M.Arch
Holocaust survivor and founder, The Azrieli Foundation

Since the end of World War II, over 30,000 Jewish Holocaust survivors have immigrated to Canada. Who they are, where they came from, what they experienced and how they built new lives for themselves and their families are important parts of our Canadian heritage. The Azrieli Foundation's Holocaust Survivor Memoirs Program was established to preserve and share the memoirs written by those who survived the twentieth-century Nazi genocide of the Jews of Europe and later made their way to Canada. The program is guided by the conviction that each survivor of the Holocaust has a remarkable story to tell, and that such stories play an important role in education about tolerance and diversity.

Millions of individual stories are lost to us forever. By preserving the stories written by survivors and making them widely available to a broad audience, the Azrieli Foundation's Holocaust Survivor Memoirs Program seeks to sustain the memory of all those who perished at the hands of hatred, abetted by indifference and apathy. The personal accounts of those who survived against all odds are as different as the people who wrote them, but all demonstrate the courage, strength, wit and luck that it took to prevail and survive in such terrible adversity. The memoirs are also moving tributes to people – strangers and friends – who risked their lives to help others, and who, through acts of kindness and decency in the darkest of moments, frequently helped the persecuted maintain faith in humanity and courage to endure. These accounts offer inspiration to all, as does the survivors' desire to share their experiences so that new generations can learn from them.

The Holocaust Survivor Memoirs Program collects, archives and publishes these distinctive records and the print editions are available free of charge to libraries, educational institutions and Holocaust-education programs across Canada, and at Azrieli Foundation educational events. They are also available for sale to the general public at bookstores. All editions of the books are available for free download on our web site at: www.azrielifoundation.org.

The Azrieli Foundation would like to express appreciation to the following people for their invaluable efforts in producing this series: Simone Abrahamson, Florence Buathier, Jesse Cohoon, Darrel Dickson (Maracle Press), Sir Martin Gilbert, Stan Greenspan, Robin Harp of the US Holocaust Memorial Museum, Richard Mozer, Arnaud Regnaud, Sylwia Szymańska-Smolkin, Keaton Taylor, Lise Viens, Margie Wolfe and Emma Rodgers of Second Story Press, and Piotr Wróbel.

About the Glossary

The following memoir contains a number of terms, concepts and historical references that may be unfamiliar to the reader. For information on major organizations; significant historical events and people; geographical locations; religious and cultural terms; and foreign-language words and expressions that will help give context and background to the events described in the text, please see the glossary beginning on page 145.

Introduction

A warm and humourous man with a precise memory for unique events in his difficult past and a way with the words, it is clear that Felix Opatowski *needs* to tell his story so many years after the events of World War II. At the same time, the relative ease with which he recounts his experiences in *Gatehouse to Hell* cannot quite allow us to forget the enormous effort it took to hold himself together while having to face, and therefore relive, the memory of the ghetto, the harsh existence in Auschwitz, the profound losses, the indescribable pain.

In telling us this story of his memories of family lost, pain and guilt, Felix warns us that "the line of sanity had been stretched to its limit" complicating, intensifying and simultaneously constraining the fullness of recall. Yet all the while, Felix manages to hold on to an array of wretched experiences filed away in his catalogue of memories during the sixty-six years since he was "liberated" from his hell, or, as Felix writes, since that moment when he "re-entered the world."

Felix Opatowki begins his memoir by asking the question: "How can anyone imagine the mental state of a survivor?" And yet, *Gatehouse to Hell* is exactly this attempt. Making optimal use of the flexible literary form that is memoir, Felix portrays his own mental state as a survivor of Auschwitz by remembering with meticulous detail all that he can, while at the same time maintaining confidence that what the survivor forgets carries with it its own kind of validity, and that his experience of both is what really matters. It is in this context that Felix uses his memories to establish a solid framework from within which he situates his experience, thereby revealing "the mental state of a survivor." He recalls camps and subcamps, labour battalions and forced marches during the worst years of Hitler's rage against Poland and Polish Jewry, against Roma, Sinti and others declared "anti-social," against Polish intellectuals and clergy, against communists and socialists, against Germany's disabled children, against gay and lesbian citizens, and many others.

Appropriately, because Felix Opatowski has chosen to use an autobiographical genre and not a historical one, his narration follows certain generic rules common to all such texts.[1] Thus, it is not surprising to find that Felix's stories and memories both corroborate and at the same time challenge other stories we have been lucky to inherit through autobiographical writing and other forms of life writing. Felix helps to amplify our knowledge about the Holocaust in particular ways, such as providing his view of the politics of the "grey zone" of camps, ghettos and forced marches where desperate human beings do not always behave honourably, a topic not easily described in earlier decades. For example, Florian Freund's study of Ebensee – the last camp Felix endured – indicates a hierarchy of prisoners in this grey zone that Felix's narrative often underscores. The citizens of Poland and the Soviet Union were treated terribly from the start, "but on the lowest rung of the ladder...stood the Jews and the gypsies."[2] Like many other Jewish narrators, most notably Primo Levi, Felix feels it is

---

1   Primo Levi understands the differences when he writes about *The Drowned and the Saved* (Trans. Raymond Rosenthal. 1986; New York: Vintage International, 1988): "I did not intend, nor would I have been able, to do a historian's work, that is, exhaustively examine the sources. I have almost exclusively confined myself to the National Socialist Lagers because *I had direct experience only of these...*" (21).

2   *Concentration Camp Ebensee: Subcamp of Mauthausen.* Trans. Max R. Garcia. 2nd Rev. Ed. Vienna: Austrian Resistance Archives, 1998.

his responsibility to describe his torment as a memorial to the many who did not make it through the same period.

Felix's ability to retell the story of turmoil is punctuated by complex interruptions and challenges – as practical as the level of his fluency in English in the early days of immigration to Canada in 1949 with his beloved wife and first child, or as fleeting as the contours of stories told to him, or qualified by oscillating personal experience, point of view and even "rumours." Opatowski quietly acknowledges that emerging from his camp experiences was "as if I were coming out of some sort of daze." He issues a challenge to scholars, in the same vein as others have done before him: we will "never know everything about the camp" he warns, "because nobody ever really knew everything about Auschwitz." And yet we all try.

The telling of Felix's story reminds us that if we are troubled by the difficulty of writing a memoir situated in the terror legislated by a state against its neighbours and its citizens, we miss out on the details of each memoirist's unique and always uneasy recounting of the Holocaust. We miss out on the different ways in which the Jewish experience of Hitler in Poland is circumscribed when remembered from the point of view of Jewish experience in the new world of Toronto, Canada. In Felix's narration we recognize the hierarchies and patterns of acquiescence and revolt among Polish Jews and others who eventually made their way to North America, Britain and elsewhere soon after the war, the ones who "made it" in honour of the "people who didn't make it," as Felix writes and, thus, as he remembers.

Felix's immigration to Canada taught him certain things about historical memory and the stages of readiness that the Canadian public traversed before it was prepared to talk about the Holocaust. He remembers that Canadians found it impossible to listen to its newest Polish immigrants, the ones who had survived the anguish that accompanied incarceration and abuse in the years between 1939 and 1945, and in the disquieting years of immigration thereafter. The social and psychological limits on his ability to communicate in the early days of "liberation" are palpable. This may be why Felix is just now publishing his memoir, years after the events when some aspects of his younger life may either elude him or alternatively sharpen in the process of writing, depending on the numerous factors involved in the remembering of traumatic pasts. Of one thing we can be sure: if details occasionally dodge a survivor's memory, every ounce of the horror Felix is able to meet head on. Survivors never forget what it felt like, as Deborah Britzman reminds us.[3]

Keeping in mind that remembering trauma is not only a shock to the narrator's memory, but also to the community's, Felix declares that he knew three languages upon arrival in Canada in 1949 – "Polish, Yiddish and German" – and yet in spite of such fluency, he found himself unable to communicate in all the important practical and deeper senses of that verb. He writes:

My wife and I and our eighteen-month-old baby arrived in Canada in April 1949 with no money, no profession and no job. Although I was fluent in Polish, Yiddish and German, I now found myself unable to communicate. Moreover, I was given the impression from everyone I met, including Jews, that it was unfashionable to be a survivor. Most people were simply not interested in learning about the concentration camps and the atrocities that occurred in them.

We have heard this before: it was unfashionable to be a survivor. Felix tells us that it is not until Elie Wiesel publishes his own memoir, *Night* (published in the USA in 1960), that the world began to take notice. Suddenly the truth was readable, communicating all that had been until now unfashionable, perhaps unspeakable. The publication of *Night*[4] coincided with the trial of Adolf Eichmann that began in

---

3 For further details, see *Lost Subjects, Contested Objects: Toward a Psychoanalytic Inquiry of Learning.* Albany: SUNY P, 1998; and Shoshana Felman and Dori Laub, *Testimony: Crises of Witnessing in Literature, Psychoanalysis, and History.* New York: Routledge, 1992.

4 *Night*, Trans. Stella Rodway. 1960; New York: Bantam, 1982.

Jerusalem in 1961 – another major turning point in the recovery of a collective memory of the Holocaust. People around Felix began to show an interest in the finer points of National Socialism's effects on the human beings who had felt it firsthand. At that point, "the world took another look at the survivors."

~

Felix Opatowski was born in June 1924 in Lodz, Poland, where his father worked in the textile trade. Polish Jews had arrived in Poland as early as the fourteenth century at the invitation of the Polish kings, and many had settled in Lodz and other urban centres in large numbers. As Sara Horowitz explains in the introduction to Henia Reinhartz's poignant Azrieli Series memoir *Bits and Pieces* "Jewish life in Poland was full of contradictions":

On the one hand, Jewish religious and cultural life had thrived there for hundreds of years. Arriving first as transient peddlers and merchants, Jews eventually settled in Poland to escape the harsh prejudices of the nearby German Empire and other regions. ...Polish Jews lived in relative peace with their neighbours. ...Over centuries, significant centres of Jewish learning and important religious and political movements had developed and flourished. ...On the other hand, Polish Jews often experienced harsh persecution, and sometimes violent attacks...at the hands of their non-Jewish Polish neighbours. ...As Polish nationalism developed after World War I, the country became increasingly less tolerant of ethnic minorities in their midst, notwithstanding guarantees in the Polish constitution to protect the rights of minorities.[5]

Polish Jewry felt both pushed away and pulled in closer by their citizenship. This tension made it easier for Hitler to march into

---

5   Sara Horowitz, Introduction to Henia Reinhartz, *Bits and Pieces*. Series 1. Toronto: The Azrieli Foundation, 2007, ii.

Poland in 1939 and plan the next stage in establishing the German *Lebensraum* (living space). Ghettoization evolved under German occupation. Lodz was the first official ghetto, set up by the Nazis in February 1940 following the German invasion of Poland on September 1, 1939. The Lodz ghetto was responsible for supplying clothes to the German army whereas the Warsaw ghetto's inhabitants worked in munitions and other aspects of war production.

We know that as part of the plan to destroy both Polish culture and Polish Jewry, the Nazis implemented policies of forced "Germanization," especially in the western incorporated territories, which included Lodz. They renamed streets and cities – so Lodz became Litzmannstadt; they overtook Polish businesses and factories, cafes and shops, posting signs that read: "Entrance is forbidden to Poles, Jews and dogs." [6]

Felix says he was lucky to be in Lodz at that time and not Warsaw because there was no fighting in Lodz, "just occupation." Throughout the narrative, Felix's optimism infuses aspects of the story, but it is never tedious, partly because it tends to avoid the maudlin. In fact, it often gives rise to humour as in this example – you can almost hear him saying, "it sure is lucky we were occupied."

Felix and his family were removed from their home in Lodz proper and sent to Baluty, the poorest part of Lodz, which was about 75 per cent Jewish even before the occupation. As time passed, wealthy Jews from other parts of Poland and Jews from abroad were deported to the ghetto resulting in disastrous overcrowding, illness, death, and increasing levels of violence among the inhabitants. Felix comments on the role of the *Volksdeutsche* – a Nazi term for ethnic Germans living in the occupied territories – in the National Socialist program of deportation and genocide in Poland. He often calls attention to members of this group cavorting around the fenced borders of the ghetto,

6   http://www.ushmm.org/education/resource/poles/poles.php

just waiting for the perfect opportunity to harass the inmates and sometimes shoot at them randomly. These men were dangerous, and even more so when Felix realized that, like his buddies, he must learn how to barter and smuggle food into the ghetto from the outside. It is during his forays into the city that Felix encounters the *Volksdeutsche* face to face – they were threatening and killed people for the fun of it. German officers also participated in the event referred to as "hunting for humans."[7]

Remarkably, Felix does not paint all enemies with the same brush, a feature of his personality that is wise and endearing. Not even all *Volksdeutsche* are evil. Captain Charentski, for example, a commander at the camp was "a decent fellow" who "might have beaten us a few times," but "was not a murderer." To discern the degrees of decent or indecent behaviour on the part of his captors at the end of this journey through "the gatehouse to hell" is remarkable. Felix's personality stands out, demands our respect and offers insight into the National Socialist machinery that evolved in different settings at different times for different purposes – but none of which was humane. At some point in 1942, for example, Governor Hans Frank declared that the policy of extermination of the Poles collided with the need for Polish and Jewish labour – that is perhaps why the strong young men, like Felix, survived the Nazi occupation.

There are many things we admire about our narrator, such as the strength of his discernment – the way he makes choices when he can and succumbs to situations when he must; the way he respects his fellow inmates and some of his captors, yet decries the system and the guards who hold it up by abusing others. We notice the way he associates the death of his pet with certain personal revelations. We have often read about various individuals, Jewish and otherwise, who did not believe Hitler could carry out an all-out attack on European

---

7   http://www.holocaustresearchproject.net/ghettos/Lodz/lodzghetto.html

Jewry and Felix is among these once-naive folks. In order to commu-nicate his awakening, he tells us about his dog, Rex, who, when Felix was a child was used as a soccer goalpost on the field – clearly Rex is a beloved, important member of his family. It is not surprising, there-fore, that Felix attaches Rex's loyalty and his fate to his own. When a German officer shoots Rex, Felix finally realizes the severity of his circumstance as a Jew and then makes literary use of Rex's death as an early signpost of Felix's awakening. The beloved dog is linked to a particular kind of memory of historical recognition.

Like a skilled novelist, Felix Opatowski's writing adopts conven-tions that we, as readers, recognize from other times, other texts. Felix is viscerally conscious of generic conventions, making use of irony, luck and reversal to foreshadow events and provide coherence to a seemingly random series of experiences. Before the momentous death of Rex, Felix is somewhat incredulous when Polish Jews de-ported from Germany back to Poland tell stories about Kristallnacht and other antisemitic atrocities: he says "some stories we believed and some we didn't." But when Rex is murdered in front of him and his younger brother, Romek, Felix now realizes that he and his family are "in for a tough time." A turning point in the narrative, a point of recognition/reversal, he writes, "That was my first real taste of Nazi brutality."

Felix experiences the full force of this recognition when he begins his eighteen-month deportation journey to Auschwitz-Birkenau, a place so profoundly horrible that Felix likens it to "another planet." When he left Auschwitz on the terrible death march punctuated by cruelty and fear on January 18, 1945, he went on to suffer even more horrific experiences in the Mauthausen, Melk and Ebensee camps in Austria. From the ghetto jail, Felix was sent to a labour camp on December 3, 1941, and then deported to Auschwitz in August 1943. Felix remembers himself as mentally tough, an attribute that he now interprets as a shield against torture, fear, chance and illness: he writes, "my only strength was in my mind." It is this aspect of Felix's character that stays with the reader – his mind is not only strong, but also from the added vantage point of the present, it is flexible, able to adjust to constant change, toil and hardship, as needed. At times Felix seems resigned to his fate, as he remembers it, and at other times, furious. Nevertheless, the truth is Felix must travel back and forth across this line in order to recreate the past for his readers. How we know about the past is not straightforward, a fact that all historians know, as does Felix Opatowski.

This brings us back to the question Felix poses for the reader in the beginning of his memoir: "How can anyone imagine the mental state of a survivor?" Ultimately, it is through Felix's heroic effort to remember all that he can in order to reveal to us his own mental state as a survivor that we are provoked to imagine precisely that. For that incredible gift we commend him, we learn from him, and we tell others.

Marlene Kadar
York University
2011

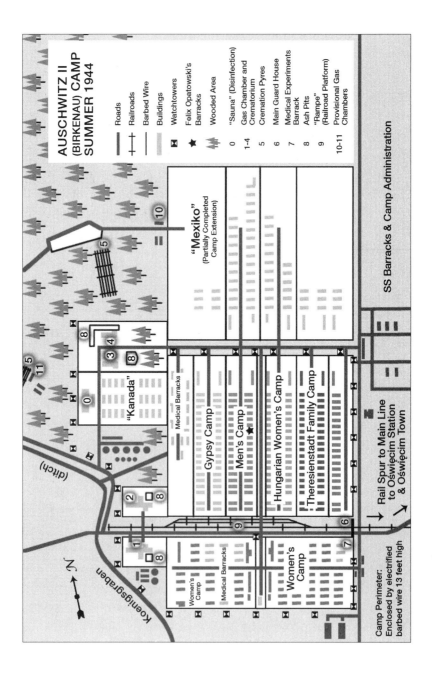

AUSCHWITZ II (BIRKENAU) CAMP SUMMER 1944

Legend:

- Roads
- Railroads
- Barbed Wire
- Buildings
- Watchtowers
- ★ Felix Opatowski's Barracks
- Wooded Area

0 — "Sauna" (Disinfection)
1-4 — Gas Chamber and Crematorium
5 — Cremation Pyres
6 — Main Guard House
7 — Medical Experiments Barrack
8 — Ash Pits
9 — "Rampe" (Railroad Platform)
10-11 — Provisional Gas Chambers

"Mexiko" (Partially Completed Camp Extension)

"Kanada"

Medical Barracks

Gypsy Camp

Men's Camp

Hungarian Women's Camp

Theresienstadt Family Camp

Women's Camp

Medical Barracks

Women's Camp

Koenigsgraben

(ditch)

N

SS Barracks & Camp Administration

Rail Spur to Main Line to Oświęcim Station & Oświęcim Town

Camp Perimeter: Enclosed by electrified barbed wire 13 feet high

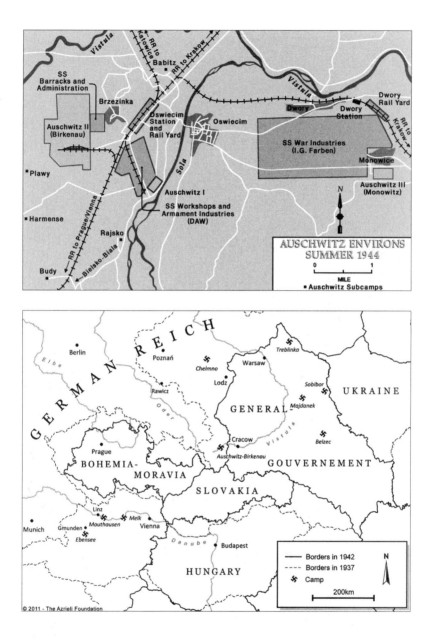

AUSCHWITZ ENVIRONS SUMMER 1944

SS Barracks and Administration

Brzezinka

Babitz

RR to Katowice

RR to Krakow

Vistula

Vistula

Dwory Rail Yard

Dwory

Dwory Station

Oswiecim Station and Rail Yard

Oswiecim

Auschwitz II (Birkenau)

SS War Industries (I.G. Farben)

RR to Krakow

Monowice

Plawy

Auschwitz III (Monowitz)

Sola

N

Harmense

Auschwitz I

SS Workshops and Armament Industries (DAW)

RR to Prague-Vienna

Rajsko

Bielsko-Biala

Budy

0   1
MILE

■ Auschwitz Subcamps

GERMAN REICH

Berlin

Elbe

Poznań

Chelmno

Warsaw

Treblinka

Lodz

Rawicz

Oder

Sobibor

UKRAINE

GENERAL

Majdanek

Prague

Cracow

Vistula

Belzec

BOHEMIA-MORAVIA

Auschwitz-Birkenau

GOUVERNEMENT

SLOVAKIA

Linz

Munich

Gmunden

Mauthausen

Melk

Vienna

Ebensee

Danube

Budapest

HUNGARY

——— Borders in 1942
- - - Borders in 1937
✠ Camp

N

200km

© 2011 - The Azrieli Foundation

The Bible tells us that he who saves a life saves the world. Jakob Artman saved my life twice and it is for this reason that I am dedicating my memoir to Jakob, Prisoner No. 141906. Unfortunately, his life was tragically taken on the eve of the fiftieth anniversary of our liberation from Auschwitz.

I am also dedicating my memoir to my beautiful wife, Regina. I was the luckiest man when I met her, the most beautiful woman I had ever seen. And today, after four kids, five grandchildren and three great-grandchildren she's just as beautiful and I still love her.

ACKNOWLEDGEMENTS:

I would like to thank the Reverend Rudy Fidel and Richard Mozer for their friendship and their support in helping me tell my story and Annette Tilden for her help with editing my manuscript.

Prologue

In 1950, five years after the concentration camps were liberated, it felt as if I were coming out of some sort of altered state; I re-entered the world in a daze and everything seemed covered in fog. It felt like there was no place to go and nowhere to turn. How can anyone imagine the mental state of a survivor? The line of sanity had been stretched to its limit.

By then, the world was again in turmoil. Stalin's Communist regime and its threatening antisemitic policies had already caused a new exodus of Jews from Eastern Europe. Among them were the Gnats, a Jewish family from Poland who had spent the war years in Siberia. They had a daughter named Regina. When I met her and fell in love in 1946, she was seventeen years old and I was twenty-two. She was the most beautiful woman I had ever seen and today, as I write down my memories after fifty years of marriage, four children and five grandchildren, I still cannot believe how fortunate I was to have met her.

My wife and I and our eighteen-month-old baby arrived in Canada in April 1949 with no money, no profession and no job. Although I was fluent in Polish, Yiddish and German, I now found myself unable to communicate. Moreover, I was given the impression from everyone I met, including Jews, that it was unfashionable to be a survivor. Most people were simply not interested in learning about the concentration camps and the atrocities that occurred in them. In my opinion, it was only when Adolf Eichmann was caught in Argentina and taken to Jerusalem for his televised trial in 1961 – and particularly when Elie Wiesel's writings were published – that the world took another look at the survivors.[1]

As I started to think about telling my own story, I was driven by a personal quest – the need to find a British prisoner of war whom I had only known in Auschwitz by his code name, the Count of Auschwitz. I have always felt that without him I would not be here to tell this story. I want to honour what he did to help the Jewish prisoners in the camp and do justice to his memory. I also want to tell my story in the hope that future generations will never forget the horrors of the Holocaust, of which I am a survivor. I know that I owe something to the people who didn't make it. These people did not commit any crimes. These people did not kill anybody. Young, old, pregnant women, babies – what could their crimes possibly be? They died solely because they were Jewish. The world must remember what happened to them so that they didn't die in vain.

Most of what I will tell you here I experienced personally or saw with my own eyes. I will also tell you some things that other people told me, and rumours that I heard. Yet, having finished this memoir, I reflect on the fact that long after the survivors, including myself, are gone, historians will continue to write about the Holocaust, especially about Auschwitz. But they will never really know everything about the camp because nobody ever really knew everything about Auschwitz.

Felix Opatowski, Prisoner No. 143425
Toronto, 2008

---

1 For information on Adolf Eichmann and Elie Wiesel, as well as on other major organizations; significant historical events and people; geographical locations; religious and cultural terms; and foreign-language words and expressions contained in the text, please see the glossary.

My Childhood in Lodz

I was born in Lodz, Poland on June 15, 1924. When I was growing up, the population of Lodz was approximately half a million and about one-third of that was Jewish. Of these, I would say that 50 per cent had something to do with textiles, one way or another.

My parents' names were Esther and Nathan. I had one brother, five years younger than me, named Romek. He was a good-looking kid with lots of blond curls. When I still had some, my hair was a reddish colour. Like many of the Jews in Lodz, my father worked in the textile trade. He was born on a farm not far from Łask, a town about fifty kilometres from Lodz. My mother, Esther, was born exactly at the turn of the century, in 1900, and she was about five years younger than my father. Back then we didn't always know people's exact dates of birth and, unlike in Canada, celebrating birthdays was not common. I don't remember the dates when my parents were born – only the years.

When my father was about fifteen years old, his father told him, "Son, if you're not going to do something with your life while you're still young, the Russians are going to take you into the army." Even though Poland was self-governing, it was still under Russian military occupation and young men were drafted into the army at the age of twenty and forced to serve for six years. Naturally, my father didn't want to be drafted, so he left Poland and went to Germany. Poland had open borders with Germany and Austria and their relations were relatively good.

While moving around from one place to another trying to find work, my father met a young German, who wasn't Jewish, named Max. Max had left home for the same reason as my father – in his case, to avoid being drafted into the German army. Of course, no one knew yet that there would soon be a war; they simply didn't want to be in the army. Max and my father became very close friends. They spent time travelling through Europe from one country to another, eventually going as far as Spain and Portugal. My father learned how to speak German fluently. When World War I broke out my father and Max stayed in Spain and Portugal to avoid the draft – Spain remained neutral and Portugal only entered the war in 1916. While they were in Portugal, they supported themselves by peddling cheap goods on the road and at a kiosk in the marketplace. When the war ended, they each returned to their parents. Nevertheless, they made a pact that whatever happened, they would remain friends.

The post-war period in Poland, and perhaps in all of Europe, was a struggle. Germany had lost the war and communism was gaining power there. My father came back to his father's farm near Łask, but after travelling all over Europe, he didn't want to become a farmer. Besides, the farm didn't even belong to the family. Polish landowners leased out their land to Jewish farmers and they had to pay a percentage of the produce to the landowner as well. My father had quite a number of brothers and sisters but not one of them wanted to work on the farm; each wanted to be independent.

When I was young my father's brothers and sisters would come around to visit and exchange information. I could always hear them talking because our place was small and there wasn't much privacy. Wherever we lived, if we had two rooms, it was a lot. One conversation I remember vividly was when my father's sister, Sarah, came to ask for advice. She had married a German Jew by the name of Nathan Krull. Because the economic situation in Poland was difficult – especially for Jews – they were looking for a better life. When my aunt asked my father what he thought of Germany or other countries as a place to live, he suggested that they go to Spain or Portugal because he knew people there. They took his advice and settled in Portugal, where they lived for many years.

Poland had become independent in 1918 but the economic situation for both Jews and Poles was even worse than before. There was terrible inflation and taxes were high. The government taxed people according to how much they thought a person should pay instead of verifying what they earned. Whenever I overheard my parents talking about problems, this seemed to be their biggest hardship – how to meet their taxation quota. They had very little money to begin with and it wasn't easy for them.

At a certain point my father's friend Max visited our family and decided to remain in Poland. My father was a smart man but he didn't have a profession so Max suggested that they form a business partnership. Max knew about machinery since his father was a machinist in a large German textile factory. Max's father helped them get two or three used textile machines and used the parts to put together one good knitting machine; with that, they started a small business manufacturing clothing in Lodz. They had a little shop and that's how they made a living. At around that same time, my father met my mother, most likely at a dance hall where young people congregated. They fell in love and got married in either 1921 or 1922.

My mother's parents had a little dairy stand in the market in Lodz where they sold milk and cheese. My mother and her sister would help their parents on market days. Later on they began selling dairy products from their home. When my parents got married, they lived in her parents' apartment and that's where I was born. My grandfather was Orthodox and I remember his grey beard and traditional black hat. I don't think I was more than three or four years old when he died, so I only remember him vaguely. My grandmother spent most of her time in bed. In those days, when people got old and a little bit sick, they just stayed in bed. My grandmother was always either in bed or in the kitchen and I remember very little about her as well. My father's parents, on the other hand, I remember vividly.

I visited my paternal grandfather's farm once or twice each year. On the high holidays – Rosh Hashanah, the Jewish New Year, and Yom Kippur, the Day of Atonement – we would always get together. It wasn't easy to travel there because we had to take a train and then a wagon. Sometimes my grandfather came to visit us by horse. He had red hair, like I did, and a thick, bushy beard. He was as strong as a bull. One time, when I was about ten, he took me to the barn and said, "There's a sack of potatoes. Can you take it into the kitchen? Your grandmother is going to need it to cook." I grabbed the sack of potatoes, but I couldn't lift it. He said, "What kind of a man are you?" He took the sack of potatoes on one shoulder, took me on the other shoulder and walked to the kitchen like that. He was big and stocky, and I remember him as a very kind man.

On my grandfather's farm there were many fruit trees and lots of bees. Whenever we went to visit there was always plenty of food and we would often bring home fruit and a pail of honey. As a child I was terribly afraid of the bees and when they chased me I would scream. My grandfather would tell me not to be afraid. He could put his hand right into the beehives and the bees didn't do anything to him. I was always amazed by this. I still don't know how he did it. There was also a stream running by the farm with lots of carp in it and my grandfather used to fish out the carp with his bare hands. Once, at dinnertime, my father asked my grandfather how he and my grandmother made a living. My grandfather said, "It's not too bad. I have a bonus. The landlord doesn't know about all the fish in the stream so I don't have to pay a percentage to him when I sell them. I make more money from the carp that I take to the city than from the fruit."

When I was a child and my brother was a baby, my grandfather gave me a little German Shepherd puppy. I was thrilled. I took the puppy home and named him Rex. This dog was my childhood companion and my whole family loved him. Wherever I went, Rex followed. He went to school with me and would wait outside until I left at the end of the day. He was so smart that he understood everything that I told him, in both Yiddish and Polish. Sometimes when my friends and I played soccer and we didn't have anything to use for a goalpost, we would use the dog instead. I would tell Rex, "Stay." And he always did. Some of the other kids were afraid to come close to the goal with Rex there and refused to play with us. It's possible that he barked at them, but Rex was never a vicious dog. Thinking back, it was really quite funny to have a dog as a goalpost.

Other good memories from my childhood are the kind that children recall when they have a happy childhood and loving parents. I remember my mother's kindness and caring. I remember how on my first day of school my mother stayed with me because I was crying and didn't want to be there without her. The teacher told her not to sit with me. "But he's crying," my mother exclaimed. What did that teacher know? I remember another mother was sitting with her child, too. The next day I didn't cry and my mother told me that I would be okay. "Don't worry, I'll be waiting outside," she said.

My mother had a sister and a brother-in-law who lived nearby and they had four children, two boys and two girls. Their younger daughter was a year or two older than me and we often played together. She was a beautiful young woman with long, red curls, but she had one problem that made her unhappy. She had freckles. I don't know who came up with the idea that girls with freckles couldn't find a husband; all I know is that everyone made fun of freckled girls and it was very disturbing for them. My cousin always felt bad that her friends had boyfriends already and she didn't.

Much of my childhood revolved around my father's little shop. It was far from where we lived and I very rarely saw my father during the week. He didn't have a car and by the time he came home from work I was already asleep. Mostly I spent time with him on Sundays when the shops were closed and I would go with him to help him clean it.

As a child I liked sports and was an avid soccer player. Soccer was very popular in Europe. At the end of our street was a huge field where most of the kids played. I was better than average and became a much sought-after soccer player. I even played on the Junior Polish League, which was a Christian team. Ultimately this saved me a lot of grief. I was once harassed by Polish hoodlums who threw stones at me and called me "dirty Jew" and "Christ-killer," and my teammates came to my defence. "Unh uh," they called out to them, "You find yourself another Jew to pick on, not him."

But even my teammates weren't always so kind to Jewish players. Jews were treated as inferior and often limited in what they could do on the team. We lived with antisemitism on a daily basis. I remember once running to my father and crying, asking him why I had been called a "dirty Jew" in the street. He replied that I was going to have to live with this problem all of my life. I couldn't understand because I was too young then, but little by little, as I became more exposed to prejudice, I began to realize what he meant. It was in the playground. It was in the school. It came from the teachers, from the principal, from everybody. I just had to resign myself to it.

School was mandatory and I went to a public school, not a separate Jewish school. Most of our teachers were Polish, but there were also some Jewish teachers. I wasn't a bad student because I was very curious and read a lot of books. I also always wanted to know a little bit more than the Polish child sitting next to me.

When I was twelve, I told my father that some of my friends were going to the Jewish high school, or *Gymnasium*, and I wanted to go too. Instead, my father advised me to go to the Catholic *Gymnasium*, where he felt I would get a better education. I registered there, but the antisemitism soon became too rough for me to handle. There were only three or four Jewish students in my class and we were treated badly. Some of the kinder Christian teachers told me that I should go to the principal to complain if I was treated unfairly. But when I went to the principal he told me not to complain and said, "You Jews shouldn't even be here." I went home upset, blaming my father for sending me to the Catholic school.

After the Christmas break, I didn't go back. Instead, I applied to another *Gymnasium* in the city. Unfortunately, though, I couldn't pass the exams to go to the next level at the new school because I hadn't yet been there a full year. What helped me get ahead was that one of the Christian teachers had seen me playing chess, which I was very good at. This teacher got to know me and helped me advance to the next grade because he knew I was bright from the way I played chess.

Although I wasn't brought up Orthodox, we had a traditional Jewish home. My family celebrated the Jewish holidays, which at that time was very rare for people who were not religious. My father, having left home early in his life, was not observant, but he knew a lot about tradition and the Bible. When I was thirteen I had a bar mitzvah. It was in what we call a *shtiebl* in Yiddish, a small synagogue. This *shtiebl* was bigger than a room; I think it had been converted from a small warehouse. I went to cheder – religious school – for a few weeks before my bar mitzvah and learned a few verses from the Torah portion that I was supposed to recite. I actually didn't learn that much because I kept sneaking out to play soccer. When the time came and I was called up to read the Torah, I said the few words that I had learned and then my mother came in with a tray of herring, a challah and a bottle of vodka. Everybody said "L'chaim!" (To life!) and that was my bar mitzvah.

Around that time I also joined a Zionist youth organization called Betar, founded by a man named Ze'ev Jabotinsky. Many Jewish children were active in youth groups. We didn't have anywhere else to go at night because we were afraid to be out in the streets. We got uniforms, played games, sang songs, and learned about Zionism and pre-state Israel – then called British Mandate Palestine. These lessons stayed with me. The Betar clubhouse was a little bit far from where I lived, but I had a friend who belonged named Jolinarsky. He was the captain of the soccer team on which I played and we all looked up to him. When he suggested I join Betar, I did. At first they wouldn't accept me because I was only thirteen, which was too young. But I kept going there and sat around and watched them until they let me stay.

Before joining Betar, I knew a little bit about Zionism from my parents. They had friends who belonged to Zionist organizations and many of these organizations arranged for guest speakers to come from British Mandate Palestine and other countries. Some of these speakers warned us that we should leave Europe. In 1938, about a year after I was with Betar, Ze'ev Jabotinsky came to Lodz on a European tour to warn the Jews that a catastrophe was approaching. At this point, not too many people spoke out so openly about their concerns. His arrival was a significant event for us since he was the founder of the Zionist Revisionist movement and played an important role in Jewish politics. When he spoke in a Jewish theatre in Lodz, it was packed with people. When he left, the crowd asked him to make another speech so he stood on top of a car and spoke some more. Members of Betar had to stand around guarding him because a rival Zionist organization tried to cause trouble and break up the meeting.

After Jabotinsky's visit I asked my father why this famous man was telling us to save our lives by going to British Mandate Palestine, or anywhere out of Europe, in fact. My father didn't answer. By that time Adolf Hitler had already written *Mein Kampf*, in which he expressed his open opposition to Jews and their "Jewish ideas" that he claimed were destroying Germany. A lot of people thought Hitler was a crackpot; but in 1935, not long after Hitler became the leader of the German people, he began implementing some of his crazy ideas through the first Nuremberg Laws. Then, after Kristallnacht – pogroms directed against German and Austrian Jews in November 1938 – Jewish leaders again warned us that we should leave Europe because war was imminent. Of course, no one could have predicted what it was really going to be like.

On September 1, 1939, Germany invaded Poland. Everyone in the apartment building came down to our place to listen to the news. Most Jews in Poland didn't have radios, but my father had purchased one just a few months before the war started – I even remember the name of the radio manufacturer, Telefunken, a German make. We did have some newspapers but not everybody could afford to buy one. I knew about what was going on mostly from what I heard other people say. I knew about Adolf Hitler from my parents, from what I heard at the Zionist youth group meetings, and occasionally I read the newspaper. I was only fifteen years old when the war broke out so I didn't really think that much about it at all. I had to do well in school, I was trying to stay out of trouble and was busy playing soccer.

I didn't realize that when war broke out it would mean the end of my schooling. I had been dreaming of going into medicine. I was fascinated by the subject. I always liked history books, too, and I enjoyed reading about the American, French and Russian revolutions. I read books by Victor Hugo, Alexandre Dumas, Pushkin, Dostoevsky and Tolstoy. I read them all before the war. When I couldn't find novels to read, I pored over medical books and technical and scientific texts. I wanted to be a doctor more than anything else.

Early on in the German occupation many of my Jewish friends mentioned that their parents were planning to pack up and move to the Soviet Union. I asked my father why we weren't doing the same. Naive as I was at fifteen, perhaps I thought this would be some kind of big adventure. My father answered, "I'm not going to run away now. I ran away once in my life and came back with nothing. I worked very hard for what I have accumulated here and I'm not going to pack up and run away again." He figured that life wasn't easy in the Soviet Union either and we would need visas and money to leave. Besides, the Germans were going to need textiles just like everyone else and since his partner, Max, was German my father thought we would be safe.

But even Max advised my father to take his family out of Poland and go to the Soviet Union. In the beginning, it was still easy to cross the border, especially at the city of Bialystok. Many Polish Jews crossed into the Soviet Union there and many of them survived. My wife's parents, for example, left with her and her two brothers and as a result they all escaped certain death. Max reassured my father that he would take care of the business and help him escape, but my father still refused.

I was very proud of my father for saying that he was not afraid to stay. I felt like he was a hero. But this was one of the first mistakes he made. My father was about forty-five years old and my mother was almost forty then. It wasn't easy for them to decide to leave everything they knew and the life they had built up for themselves. Nobody could imagine what was coming. Who in his right mind, in 1939, could think of what the future was going to be for the Jews of Europe? By the time my parents did decide to leave, it was already too late.

The War Begins

The Germans occupied Lodz on September 8, 1939, a week after the war broke out. They came through the city like a big parade, waving German flags. Everybody was standing in the streets watching the German army march through. I wasn't sure exactly what was going to happen but I knew it wasn't going to be good because I had heard how my parents and their friends were talking about the situation. Some people left for Warsaw, which was a mistake because the German air force was strafing the highways and Warsaw was getting hit worse than all the other cities. Most people had to turn back and those who made it to Warsaw probably lost their lives in the fighting that went on there. In Lodz there was no fighting, just occupation.

My very first encounter with the German occupation was when a couple *Volksdeutsche* boys came around while I was playing soccer with my friends. These *Volksdeutsche* were Poles of German ancestry whose parents had either married Poles or had come to Poland years before, when Poland belonged to Germany. We recognized the boys because they were wearing Swastika armbands and since the *Volksdeutsche* lived among us they recognized us as Jews. They told the Polish boys I was playing with, "You'd better tell these Jewish guys to get out of here. They're not supposed to play with you."

My teammates answered, "What's this got to do with anything, Jews and non-Jews playing together. These are our friends. We've been playing together all our lives." My Jewish friends and I didn't say anything. We left and never went back. They were threatening us and we were afraid. That was my first experience with Nazism.

By the first week of November, the Nazis ordered all Jews to wear a yellow armband. Two weeks later, that law was amended so that we had to wear a Star of David on every piece of clothing and were not supposed to go out without it. There were notices in the streets saying we could be fined or sent to prison; later, we heard that we might even be executed for not wearing one. Wearing the badge didn't bother me much; my mother sewed the star on my outer clothing and I went out. For my parents, however, wearing the Star of David had a terrible impact. They were ashamed to be seen in the street with a badge. I embarrassed my mother by reminding her to put on the Star of David before she went out. They just didn't want to do it.

A few times, I went out to shop for groceries with my father. We had to get food somehow, but we weren't allowed to go into a store wearing the Star of David. Besides, even if a Pole wanted to sell bread to us, he could get into trouble. So a few times, I went out without the badge. There was no choice. My parents warned me that I could get beaten up or shot, but I insisted on going.

On one occasion when I tried to stand in a lineup for bread, a *Volksdeutsche* recognized me as a Jew. "There is no bread for you Jews," he said and I was kicked out of line. No one cared if Jews didn't eat. I returned home empty-handed and wept. We really felt the bitterness and the hatred then. We had been exposed to antisemitism before, but not that kind of antisemitism.

When they needed workers, the Nazis would line people up on the street with the help of the *Volksdeutsche*. A few times they caught me and my father and made us unload their trucks and clean out their quarters. They held us for a day and sent us home at night. There was no violence or beatings yet. We just worked for the day while someone kept an eye on us. At one point while we were working, I looked at my father's face and he appeared to be angry – more at himself than at what they were making us do. On that particular day the Nazis had taken a truckload of us to work far away and then left us there. It took us two or three hours to walk home in the cold and it was starting to snow. My father mumbled to himself that he should have listened to people and taken their advice to leave when we could. I didn't know what to think. I just felt sort of claustrophobic every time we got rounded up. We were under the gun but no one had started firing yet.

By the end of 1939, although we didn't know it at the time, the Germans had started making plans for a ghetto. In February, they announced where the Jews would be relocated. In Lodz there was a section called Baluty where the conditions were much worse than ours. My family didn't live extravagantly, but at least we were in the centre of the city and managed not too badly. Baluty was a slum and the people who lived there were very poor. I would say 75 per cent of the population there was Jewish. This is where the Germans placed the ghetto.

In the early spring of 1940, we were evacuated from our apartment building. First, a big sign was posted in the hallway and the superintendent told everybody that the Jewish people had to move out. Then, one evening, a German came in with a *Volksdeutsche* to help him and they gave us verbal notice to leave the premises. I think they gave us two or three days to move out, which was a lot because I heard from other friends that they had only been given a few hours. We could only take with us what we could carry and fit in a handcart and then we were sent off to Baluty.

On the day we had to evacuate, a German officer came to our apartment to check it out and see if it was a good place to live. The officers were housed in the nicest apartments evacuated by Jews while the ordinary soldiers got the inferior ones. The officer saw Rex and patted him on the head. "Oh, what a beautiful dog," he said in German. Rex had grown to be quite handsome. His ears stood straight up like a purebred and although he wasn't that big, he was very muscular. The German noticed that whenever we spoke to Rex, he understood.

He asked his name and I told him. By that time we had to leave. My father had managed to get a handcart and was afraid they were going to take it away from us if we didn't hurry.

My father put everything together on the cart and tied it down. I was carrying something and my little brother and my mother also had a few things as we were gathered together to leave. Rex, of course, started to follow us but the German officer called out to Rex to stay with him. Rex didn't move. I tried to take him along but the officer wanted to keep him. He held Rex back until Rex started growling at him.

"You'd better keep Rex quiet," my father whispered to me. I was too young to understand the danger of refusal. The German asked my father for a leash but we had never had a leash for Rex. Instead he tied a rope around his neck. There was a little bit of a struggle, but Rex wasn't fierce. He never bit people. As we left, my brother, Romek, was crying and I was crying too as the German held Rex back from us. "Just quiet down," my father told us. "Whatever he wants, he can take." We had already had plenty of opportunities to see what happened if someone talked back to a German soldier.

We started walking toward Baluty. My mother had some relatives there but I didn't know them well. Baluty was not really in walking distance and when I was a child we hardly ever used the streetcar to visit people – it was expensive and it didn't go many places. Now we had no choice but to walk. It probably took about two hours to get to my mother's cousins, especially since we were carrying so much with us. It wasn't so easy for my mother to remember exactly where her cousins lived either because she hadn't been there in so long.

We only stayed with our relatives for a little while. It was very cramped and we weren't particularly welcome there since we hadn't had much to do with them before. Nevertheless, the Jews living in Baluty had been given orders to share accommodations with any friends or relatives. Most people would rather share with family than with strangers. It's possible that our relatives took us in because they felt sorry for us, but I think it was also for more materialistic reasons. I'm sure my father gave them some money.

Our cousins lived in a small apartment. I seem to remember them having only two rooms and a kitchen. They had two or three children, there were four of us, and soon another family moved in as well. The mother of the new family was my mother's cousin and closest friend. They had two boys. There must have been at least twelve people living in those two small rooms. Later, even more people arrived. Somehow we all lived together, but we could hardly get into the kitchen. We slept on the floor and I had to sleep on the landing outside the apartment. Sometimes, if I wasn't careful, I fell down the stairs, but luckily there were only five or six steps so the fall wasn't too far.

After about a month or so my father found us another place to live close by. My parents didn't tell me why we were moving. Maybe it was too cramped and uncomfortable, or possibly my cousins were charging too much and my father didn't have enough money to pay them. Who knows? Our new place, however, was much more comfortable. It had belonged to Poles who were evacuated from Baluty to make room for the Jews. I'm sure they didn't want to leave, but all of the Christians had been forced out of the ghetto area. All of a sudden we had a whole house to live in and the former residents had even left some potatoes in the cellar. What a picnic for us!

In the very beginning, life in the ghetto wasn't so bad because people were still bringing in provisions. The ghetto wasn't blocked off until the end of April 1940, so until then we could still leave the ghetto in the daytime if we had a permit. Taking a chance – because Jews weren't allowed to use public transportation – my father sometimes went by streetcar to see his partner, Max, and he never came home empty-handed. Max was kind to him and said he would help him any way he could. Although the Nazis decreed that Jews couldn't own property or run businesses, Max made sure that my father still got his share of the profits. A few times he even came to the ghetto on bicycle to bring us food. One night I overheard my father telling my mother, "I'm not going to see Max any more. I think he gives me his own bread. I can't go to him and take away his bread because I don't know if he has enough for himself." They were that close.

The situation in the ghetto deteriorated rapidly and soon became so terrible that we didn't dwell on these things. More than 150,000 people were forced to live in Baluty, and people continued arriving from the towns and little villages surrounding Lodz. As more people were transferred to the ghetto, living there became increasingly chaotic. Although it was so overcrowded, at least some people had money and there were provisions. The overcrowding got even worse in the fall of 1941, when wealthy Jews from outside Poland arrived in the ghetto and the ghetto population grew to more than 200,000. Jews from Germany, Czechoslovakia and Austria were all being sent to Lodz. Many of them were better off than the Polish Jews and brought valuables with them. Some of them had gold, diamonds and fine clothes. Before long they had to sell everything they owned because they had nothing to eat, but there wasn't enough food to go around. Bread became even scarcer than money.

Although we always had trouble getting food, it was still manageable until the Germans closed the ghetto. Then the problems really started. They took away our Polish money and printed special ghetto money that we got if we did special work. But where were we going to get work when there were so many people in one place? The only work we had was organized by Chaim Rumkowski, head of the Jewish Council, also called the Judenrat. Before the war, Rumkowski had been the head of an orphanage. When the Germans appointed the Lodz Judenrat they put Rumkowski in charge, whether he wanted the job or not. The Judenrat had the responsibility of providing services like health and housing for the ghetto population and organizing distribution of food, work details, the Jewish police and the fire department. Rumkowsi didn't have any idea what to do at first, but he ended up organizing labour in the ghetto very well. He organized work for the war effort so well that the ghetto lasted until August 1944.

The German authorities started establishing forced labour factories. When they needed people to work in them, they came to Rumkowski. He was happy to give them workers because he expected that they would be fed in exchange for their work and there would be fewer people to feed in the ghetto. Rumkowski also thought that if he could get enough contracts for the German war effort, Germany would keep the Jews in the ghetto alive. Unfortunately, the Germans had a different idea – they didn't want any Jews alive, even if they needed them. That was the goal of the Nazis.

One night when I was sleeping, I felt something lick my face. I opened my eyes and a dog jumped on top of me. Rex had run away from the German officer and had sniffed out where we lived! I couldn't believe it. We had moved twice in the ghetto and he still managed to find us. After being with that dog so many years, I still hadn't realized how really clever he was. Rex sniffed around and found my mother and father sleeping in another corner. Everybody got up and we made such a hoorah. Then my mother said, "How are we going to feed him? We don't even have any table scraps." We were eating scraps ourselves. So I said, "I'm going to give him mine," and my brother said, "I'm going to give him mine too." We were so happy.

A couple of weeks later, the German who stole Rex drove into the ghetto on a motorcycle. Not every German soldier could enter the ghetto and finding out where we lived was not easy. But he found us and came around. When he saw Rex, he took out his pistol and shot the dog right in front of us. That was my first real taste of Nazi brutality. I started to cry but my mother told me to stop. She was scared that the German was going to shoot me too. My brother and I took Rex and buried him in a nearby field.

Now I really realized that we were in for trouble. The Polish Jews we knew who had lived in Germany and were deported back to Poland after the Kristallnacht pogrom in 1938 had told us stories about the Nazis. Some we believed and some we didn't, but little by little we began to suspect what the Germans wanted to do with us. When that

German officer shot my dog, I knew we were in for a tough time. I realized that all those stories we heard about the Nazis were true.

German officers came to the ghetto every few days to round up people for work. In the beginning, the people they took went to work in areas close to Lodz and then returned to the ghetto at night. But by the end of 1940, they started deporting people to forced labour camps.

In the ghetto, there were houses that had been destroyed and needed repairs, which was hard work. I didn't do that work myself, but when houses were demolished, I was fast enough to steal a piece of wood to trade for bread. That was the beginning of my activities in the trade business. Once in a while I would also find something to bring home from the area of the ghetto that had been evacuated by the Poles since there was often something to steal there. That was all I did. I was still active in playing soccer, but little by little, when we had less food and sometimes no food, I had to stop playing soccer because I didn't have the energy anymore.

When the winter of 1940 set in, we needed fuel for warmth and cooking. Almost immediately, wood became just as scarce as bread. We couldn't find coal or wood and if we could find any, we had to pay good money for it. We demolished furniture just to cook a meal.

Finally, in the dead of winter, we had nothing left at all. My father looked for work, but it wasn't easy to find. My mother cried because she couldn't feed us. My brother cried from hunger. Then one day my father came home with a loaf of bread. A loaf of bread! It felt like a holiday. Then I found out that he had joined a work detail, or *Kommando*, called the *Scheisskommando*. They would remove human waste from the toilets and sewers because in Lodz, the apartments, especially in the poor district, had only outdoor plumbing. When they emptied the outhouses and the public washrooms they had to move the excrement out of the ghetto to dispose of it. When I saw my father doing this work, he pretended not to see me. He was ashamed for his family to know what he was doing, but that was the

only work he could find. By now we were starving, so it was better than nothing. Later on, the people who had shied away from this
kind of work couldn't even get that. It was considered a "prominent"
job because workers got extra pay and special rations for it.

Jolinarsky, the soccer captain who had taken me to the Betar
Zionist organization, was also in the ghetto. When I was still playing
soccer in the ghetto, before I got too weak, Jolinarsky took me aside
one day and gave me a piece of stale bread. Oh, I tell you, this piece
of stale bread sure tasted good. I probably hadn't eaten for two or
three days, which was common – to eat every day was practically impossible. I started gobbling it down quickly until at the last second I
remembered my little brother. Romek was just as hungry as me. I left
one piece in my pocket, went home and gave it to Romek. He looked
at me incredulously, wondering how I got it. I told him, "Just eat it up
and don't ask questions."

The next time I saw Jolinarsky I asked him where he had gotten
the bread. He told me that the lack of food in the ghetto had forced
people to start smuggling, with some ghetto residents selling bread or
potatoes to others in exchange for whatever valuables they still had.
Then they'd sneak out of the ghetto into the area where the Poles were
still living and exchange these valuables for more food. Jolinarsky was
one of these smugglers. "There are a few guys I know who can get out
of the ghetto," Jolinarsky told me. "If you come with me this evening,
I'll show you what to do."

I knew this was dangerous and I could get shot for sneaking out of
the ghetto. Jolinarksy told me that he was almost shot himself. On the
other hand, I had seen my father doing the *Scheisskommando* work
and felt I'd rather take a chance at being shot than let my father keep
doing it for a little extra soup or bread. And so I started smuggling.

The first time I brought food home my mother wanted to know
where I got it. "Did you steal it?" she asked. "Mother, don't ask questions," I answered. "I have some food. Eat something first." I thought
with a little extra food, she'd be happy. When my father came home,

she showed him what I had brought. Potatoes, bread, even a piece of butter. They asked where I got the food, but they weren't dummies. They knew there was smuggling going on. At first my father protested – he was afraid I would get killed. Then he stopped asking about it.

The ghetto was fenced in with plain ordinary barbed wire or with wooden fences and a bit of wire. Police guarded the fence, but the area was so large that there were always places left unguarded. To carry out our smuggling we had to wait until it was dark and find places where we could sneak under or over the wire to the other side where the Poles who lived nearby knew us and knew that we wanted to trade goods for food. Mostly we got bread, potatoes, butter and cheese, which we paid for with jewellery, gold or other valuables. I had no clue what these items were worth, but Jolinarsky was teaching me what to do.

When my father saw I wasn't going to stop smuggling, he began to help out. He went to some friends and told them that he could get them food if they gave him valuables. I didn't want my father to be involved in case something went wrong, but I didn't have a choice. He was the only man I could trust and I had to trust somebody. Some of the other parents helped out too, so at least we managed to organize a way to get food into the ghetto.

Then, one day, me and a few other boys got caught. As we were nearing the fence outside the ghetto a German guard started yelling. He shone lights on us and began shooting. We ran and one of my friends was hit. I don't remember if he was killed, but he fell down. Two of us managed to get over the fence. I jumped over the wire and started running. The Jewish police inside the ghetto were also on guard and they caught us, which was lucky. If they hadn't, the Germans would have killed us. This way, when they saw the Jewish police capture me and the other boys, the German guards stopped chasing us and stayed on the other side of the wire fence. Since we gave them extra food, the Jewish police often looked the other way when it came to smuggling. It didn't matter who they were, they didn't get very much to eat either. This time, however, they arrested me, Jolinarsky and the other guys and took us to the jail.

The commander of the jail, who was Jewish, appeared to be a senior officer. He walked around with a hat and a special uniform. The jailers wore ordinary police uniforms but the commander looked like a big shot. Such stupid things like this are what I remember. Living conditions in the jail were awful. I was thrown in with murderers and thieves. It was crowded and there weren't any beds, so we slept on the floor. The only thing that wasn't so bad was that we got a daily ration of food. If there were enough turnips, they gave us turnips. If there were enough potatoes, they gave us potatoes. It was never really consistent but I had more food in the jail than outside of it. My parents came to visit me several times. One time my mother brought me some carrots because, in the summer, they could still grow vegetables.

I was in the ghetto jail for almost six months. I remember, while I was in there, hearing about the German invasion of the Soviet Union, which was in June 1941. In early December, the Nazis started transporting people from the ghetto jail to labour camps in the Poznań area, about two hundred kilometres northwest of Lodz. The commander of the jail gave a speech about how we were going to be transported to a camp that was better than the ghetto, where we'd be fed, and that we should take postcards to send home to our family. The Jewish police came around to threaten that some of us were going to be interrogated by the Germans. Then German officers did come and take some of the inmates. Maybe they shot them. I never found out.

For some reason, my mother learned about the transports before I did. Someone had let her know that I would be going to a labour camp and before we all left my mother and my brother came to say goodbye. She brought me a jacket and some personal items like a shirt and undershirt and an extra pair of shoes. The most important thing she brought me was a blanket and a pillow – these items became very useful in the labour camp. That was the last time I saw my mother and my brother.

On that very last day in jail my father didn't come to visit. I never saw my family again and I never heard from them again. It was only after the war that I found out why my father hadn't visited me that day.

Weisser Adler

Early on the morning of the transport, the Germans assembled us in a big field outside of Lodz. There must have been more than three thousand people gathered there. The Germans were selecting the younger men for the labour camps. I saw lots of women on the other side of the field waiting to be transported, too. They sent the women away from the field, but I don't know where they went.

Before we set out, they gave us each half a loaf of bread, which we were very happy to get. They told us this bread had to last until we reached the camp, but half a loaf of bread doesn't last very long. We went to the first labour camp in a civilian train. Poznań was the head office for several of the camps in the area and our first stop was at Poznań Stadium. I saw very little of it, but I remember that there were trucks waiting there with workers in uniforms. They took our names and they put us on the trucks to be sent to different destinations. Some people remained in Poznań. My group was taken to a camp in the town of Rawicz, about one hundred kilometres from Poznań, known to us as Weisser Adler (White Eagle), the name of the school it was housed in. It was an awful camp with terrible conditions. I spent almost two years there.

Weisser Adler had been converted from a school. It was large enough to accommodate two thousand people or so, all squeezed together. The sleeping quarters were made up of long bunks in three tiers. They put straw on the bare boards and we slept on the straw with whatever belongings we had. My blanket and pillow came in very handy because they didn't give us any blankets. There was also one big washroom and one huge room where we ate.

Whenever we needed help, more workers were sent from Poznań. These people were sent out from the ghetto, and the labour camp and ghetto administration were paid for all our work. The only pay we received was a bit of lousy food.

The commander of the camp was an ethnic German, a *Volksdeutsche*, who had been an officer in the Polish army. His name was Charnetski and we called him Captain Charnetski. He was a decent fellow, but very strict. He might have beaten us a few times, but he didn't hit too hard and he was not a murderer. He wasn't out to kill anybody. One good thing about him was that he tried to run the camp in a military fashion. He disapproved of the starvation conditions and complained to the German officials who came once a month to do an inspection that we didn't have enough food. He didn't like the fact that a lot of us were dying. As long as we were alive, those who ran the camp got paid. Then again, they didn't give us enough food to keep us alive. It was a no-win situation.

One thing that Captain Charnetski was very strict about was forcing us to wash, even in the winter. When we got up to go to work, each one of us had to get undressed to the waist and wash in cold water at the pump. Charnetski would often watch us and noticed if somebody was just splashing himself or actually washing. He would give over the names to the foremen and when we came back from work, anyone who didn't wash wouldn't get supper. So we learned the proper routine very quickly. It only took one time of being denied food and, believe me, we didn't refuse to wash anymore. We thought he just wanted to torture us, but I'm sure that this saved some lives; when we washed ourselves with cold water, we got toughened up. We developed a kind of armour from the experience. It wasn't pleasant at five o'clock in the morning, but it was good for hygiene since there was nowhere else to shower or bathe. I got so used to the cold water in the morning that later I missed it.

At the labour camp I met two Czech brothers, very fine, intelligent men, who were a little older than me. One of them had been a professor. They talked to me as if I understood the things they knew. There were times I'd have to ask them to slow down because I didn't know what they were talking about. For instance, one time they were discussing Sigmund Freud. "You don't know who Sigmund Freud is?" they asked in astonishment. They were stunned that I didn't know who he was. I mean, how would I know about Freud? He was obviously a very famous man, but I was only a teenager and I didn't have much education. Yet, I always asked questions, wherever I was.

There were quite a few intelligent people in the camp – teachers, professors, doctors and surgeons – and because they had nothing better to do when I asked them questions, they answered me. We were all suffering from beatings and hunger and lice and it was difficult to fall asleep, so we talked. I always had a thirst for knowledge and I was especially interested in religion. I found out more about the topic in the labour camps than I had known in all the years previously because of these people. At night, we had to talk very low to avoid disturbing others. Some people got killed for that.

The labour camp wasn't a good experience, but it was an experience.

The work was incredibly hard. The hours were very long and we worked far away from the camp. It didn't matter how much time it took us to get to work, we still had to put in the same amount of hours at the job. We got a piece of bread in the morning and a little soup in the evening. Mostly the Germans took us to repair highways. Polish roads were lousy. I don't think the Nazis had enough manpower or money to build new highways so we were widening the existing ones. They made new lanes on both sides because they needed transportation for the military supplies they were taking from Germany to the Soviet Union. It was very strenuous work.

Every morning we had to wake up early to make it to work by seven. Yet, every time we finished a kilometre or two of road, we were further and further away from the camp. One time we were so far away that it took us hours just to get back. By the time we arrived at the camp we were so exhausted that we could hardly even eat the soup for which we had starved the whole day. The next morning we were up again by five o'clock but couldn't make it there for seven because it was too far, so the next day we had to get up even earlier.

The tools that we had were primitive. If they had fed us decently, hadn't beaten us and given us decent tools, we could have finished the work in half the time. But the Germans didn't care. People were collapsing on the way to work or in the middle of the job. Either they got a bullet in the head or they just lay where they fell. They couldn't move anymore.

When the highway was finished they drove us to our next job because it was too far away to walk. We were assigned to work on the Vistula River, the main river for transportation. In some places the river wasn't wide enough for supply boats to pass through. They took us to those spots where the river was narrow and muddy and we waded through the river the whole day, digging out slime, rocks and bushes, and then reinforcing the banks. We never tried to resist. We weren't organized and we were too weak. We hardly had the strength to crawl up the banks that we were reinforcing.

Some of us were assigned to move the dirt and rocks away from the river with wheelbarrows and that was even harder work. The guards switched us around every few hours but because I was one of the youngest ones, I had to push the wheelbarrows most of the time. If the wheelbarrow tipped over in the muck, I was in real trouble since the overseers, who were mostly *Volksdeutsche*, thought it was sabotage. We tried to help each other out because if one of us fell down with a wheelbarrow we could be beaten to death. Whenever work was interrupted, they beat us. Even worse, if we were hit over the head with a shovel or whatever, we didn't have any way to recover.

We had to go on working when we were in pain. If we couldn't do our work properly we didn't get supper. It was like a domino effect. When we didn't get food, the next day we could barely work; a lot of us died.

I saw some people before they died from hunger. Other men called this type of person a *Muselmann*. It took me a long time to understand what a *Muselmann* was. I don't know where the term really came from, but somebody explained it to me like this: a Muslim man (*Muselmann* in German) wears a white turban on his head; if the people who were dying had a towel or a shirt, they wadded it up and put it on their heads like a turban because they were feverish. Most of the time they would wander around in a daze, not knowing what was happening to them. These people stumbled around, starving, while still holding pieces of bread in their hands. That was the kind of shape they were in. I remember, when I got out of bed one morning, I said to one of these fellows, "Are you coming out?" There was no answer. A piece of bread was lying beside him. He had just given up. He was still moving, but he was finished. I thought to myself, "No way. I'm not going to end up like this."

One time I saw a man who was so weak from starvation that he got dizzy and fell down, so they beat him to death. We were beaten all the time. It wasn't necessary, but the guards enjoyed doing it. They also hung a few men. That was just how it was.

In the beginning, we didn't know about the Nazis' plans to murder the Jews. We just knew we were in a labour camp. We thought we were going to work and that at least they were going to feed us decent food so we could work. But as it turned out, even at the camps where the labourers worked on building rockets for the Germans, the Germans starved them all to death when they no longer needed them. We asked ourselves, "Why?" It was a big "why."

We soon realized that it was going to be impossible to live and work on the pitiful rations we received, so we started a smuggling operation like the one I was involved in at the ghetto. At night, Weisser Adler had only two guards and the commander. It wasn't barricaded with electric wire because there was no place for us to go. There were some Polish farms around there, but a Pole wasn't likely to take us in because it was too dangerous. He might give us some food, though. Since there was only one German guard at the front entrance we could jump out the back windows of the school to leave the camp. We knocked at various farmers' doors and some of them took pity on us and gave us some food, mostly vegetables, carrots and potatoes. We were happy with a potato even if it was raw. Some farmers didn't have anything to give us. A few times, people got caught, and several men were beaten up and put into solitary confinement for a few days without food.

There were a few months when we were contracted out to a big farm to harvest sugar beets. We ate the sugar beets even though they didn't taste very good. It helped our hunger a little bit. The beets were dark on the outside but when we peeled off the skins they were white on the inside. At first when we bit into them they were sweet, just like sugar, but in a matter of seconds they became bitter. Sometimes they were so bitter that we couldn't even swallow them. At that time, we still had our belongings, so many of us had knives to cut off the skin on the beets. I didn't have a knife, but I borrowed one when I needed it. The Germans weren't afraid that we would attack them; they weren't afraid that we would retaliate.

Once in a while, the guards told us we could write postcards and they would mail them for us. We wrote postcards to our families in the ghetto, but when we didn't get any replies, we asked the guards what happened. They said that the situation in the ghetto was so bad that they didn't allow people there to send any packages or mail. Once, they told us that we didn't get any replies because we didn't deserve such privileges. I think the only reason they told us to write postcards was because they wanted to tease us. Some of the guards were Poles who were probably nobodies before the war and all of a sudden they had a stick or a gun and they could do whatever they wanted. They were arrogant and cruel.

Hundreds of us disappeared very, very quickly. People were dying daily. Before the camp, I had never known what hemorrhoids were. But while there, I learned that some people died just from hemorrhoids that started to bleed and wouldn't stop. There were no medical facilities at all. If we got injured, the only medication was cold water. There was one Jewish fellow who had attended medical school and kind of served as a nurse. He was the only one who could examine us to say if we were well enough to go to work or not. He got strict orders from the camp commander that someone had to be really sick to be excused.

Our sleeping conditions were so terrible that it wasn't long before the straw became infested with lice. They were eating us alive. When the commander found this out he immediately sent us for delousing. The guards took us in trucks to a convent where the nuns, who were also nurses, were paid for delousing. They took us in, stripped us of our clothes and led us to a machine where they sprayed us with a special kind of green liquid solution. It burned so terribly that we yelled out in pain. It wouldn't have hurt so much if we hadn't already scratched up our bodies to relieve the itching from the lice bites.

Once our clothes were disinfected we got dressed, but as we were putting on our clothes, the nuns saw how awful we looked and became concerned. When they found a chance, they gathered together what they could and gave us some bread. They were so kind to us – I don't think those nuns even had enough food for themselves. They probably gave away their own portions.

The delousing took three full days. While we were gone they changed the straw in the bunks and washed everything. When we returned, another group was sent to the convent. While the hygienic conditions became a little bit better, it didn't take long until the lice were back. On the other hand, by then only half of us were left alive so the sleeping quarters weren't quite so congested. Eventually there weren't enough of us to do the required work and the Germans dissolved the Weisser Adler labour camp. They transferred us to another labour camp – where many people had also died – and combined both to form a satellite camp, which was nearby and was also surrounded by farms.

On the way to this camp, several men tried to run away, but the guards caught them and put them in jail. They hung five or six of them and the whole camp was ordered to watch. That took care of any more escape attempts. That was the first hanging I ever witnessed. I was very disturbed and had nightmares because of it. Before they were hanged, the men yelled out, "Let Poles live! Down with the Germans!" The Poles thought this was a very patriotic thing to do and later they put up a monument for them. It's too bad I don't remember where it is because when I went back to Poland later, I wanted to visit it.

After the hanging, the entire camp was punished. The commander didn't feed us for three days, yet we had to work just the same. We got coffee but no food. The punishment didn't stop some of us from sneaking out to the farms to look for something to eat. Mind you, there were men who resented us for going since we weren't only putting ourselves in danger, but all of them as well. Nevertheless, when we came back we always shared whatever we had with them.

The inmates from the camp we joined were also from Lodz. I think they must have been sick even before we arrived. None of them looked very healthy to us – we thought we didn't look too bad in comparison. After about four weeks, a typhus epidemic broke out and half of the camp died. I think only a few hundred remained alive by the end of our time there.

Typhus was not a sickness that a person could identify right away. Generally, people start getting weak and dizzy and fall asleep. Some of the inmates didn't even have time to crawl into their bunks because the sickness hit them so quickly and severely. I was lying in my bunk when it hit me. I must have been unconscious for at least a week. The only thing the ones who weren't so sick could do for us was to give us water. Even while we were unconscious, they tried to give us water to drink.

Both the sick and the healthy slept in the same place. Some of the sick got up; some of them didn't. A few inmates, when they got better, started moving out the dead bodies. Even some of the Germans who were guarding the camp were exposed and got sick too. I mean, typhus doesn't discriminate. I heard that two Germans died, but I don't know if they died or if they went to the hospital.

When I regained consciousness, I was very thirsty because the fever had been so high. Somebody had brought me water, but it wasn't enough. When I first tried to get out of my bunk, I collapsed. Finally I managed to crawl over to the water pump. While I was there I saw a man coming down the stairs from the floor above. He was eating a handful of grain. I asked him where he got it. "Go upstairs and get some of it yourself," he said. I hadn't known that on the second floor was a warehouse, or as we called it in German, a *Magazine*. I wondered how I would get up there. I could hardly move and had trouble enough dragging myself to the pump. "Maybe when I get a little bit better," I thought to myself.

For dinner that night we were given some decent soup. At least we found a few potatoes in it. I felt as if my blood was beginning to flow again, and I started feeling a little bit warmer. The tips of my fingers had been cold and numb. That night, I tried to crawl up the stairs, but I just couldn't. The next morning, I made it up one flight. On the landing there was raw rice and barley, which I ate. It was filling but gave me a stomachache.

The following day we got more soup and I felt a little bit better. I thought, "If there's grain on the first level, I'm going to climb up another flight and see what's there." And guess what? I found sugar. I couldn't believe it. Sugar! I started eating it – then my heart really started pumping. I scooped it up and filled every pocket I had. I was afraid I would be caught. The Germans knew that some of us had found the barley and the rice but they really didn't make a big effort to take it away. Maybe they felt a little bit sorry for us after all. Needless to say, one of the cooks complained, "If you guys eat the grain raw, I'll have nothing to cook with." But nobody knew about the sugar.

I mentioned what I had found to a few other fellows and they went to get some sugar, too. That sugar was such a boost for us. About a week later many of us were well enough to start working again. Somehow, the conditions weren't so bad anymore. Nobody was shooting us. Nobody was coming in and beating us just because we were Jews. We were only punished if the commander thought we really deserved it.

Once in a while we got a little bit of news about the war from the Polish people we met when we were sent to work on farms. The Polish farms were not as industrialized as Western farms and their irrigation methods were not as advanced. They had to depend on rain to fill their irrigation ditches and when there were floods, they constantly needed to repair the ditches. They probably paid the commander for a few hundred labourers from the camp to help them. That was the only time we hoped they would take us out to work because the farmers gave us food and information.

In 1942, the news on the front was good for the Germans – which was not such good news for us. Rumours started spreading that the labour camps were going to be shut down. Nobody knew what was going to happen to us. After the war, I learned that in January 1942, high-ranking Nazis such as Reinhard Heydrich and Adolf Eichmann had assembled to discuss a new plan for a "Final Solution to the Jewish Question." All of the ghettos and labour camps were to be dissolved. A year and a half later, in the summer of 1943, the Germans closed our camp.

When I had first left the ghetto in the transport from Lodz, there were approximately 2,500 to 3,000 of us. When I left Weisser Adler for the next camp, only about three to five hundred people were left. The rest had died of starvation, beatings, overwork and typhus. The labour camps were bad enough. We didn't think anything could be worse, but unfortunately we were wrong. They put us in cattle cars on trains and sent us to Auschwitz.

We didn't know where we were going, of course, but a few Polish labourers who had worked with us for pay told us, "If you have a chance to escape before they take you to Auschwitz, you'd better do it, because there's no escape from Auschwitz." That was the first time I'd heard of Auschwitz. It was what the Germans called the small Polish town of Oświęcim, but I didn't know anything else about it. I was in a cattle car full of people and nobody knew where we were going.

In August 1943, I was part of a transport of about two thousand people, maybe more. We got a portion of bread and a little water when we got on the train. The trip took a few days because they picked up a few hundred of us, then they went to other camps and picked up more. At these stops, they wouldn't let us out, but I could see that they were packing more wagons with Poles and Roma, called Gypsies at the time, but mostly with Jews. There were so many camps; by the last stop I couldn't believe there were so many of us crammed into each wagon. We had to make the best of the sleeping arrangements. We didn't get any water on the way.

Before we left for Auschwitz, I'd had dysentery for a couple of weeks. Dysentery was very common and there was nothing we could do for it. Having dysentery was no picnic. Toilet paper was out of the question. And we were on the train for a few days with no place to relieve ourselves. There was only one bucket. The people who knew about dysentery told us not to drink and to eat as little as we could, but once we were on the train we didn't get anything to eat or drink for a couple of days anyway.

Auschwitz

We arrived at the Auschwitz station at night. I don't know what time it was but it was dark. A very curious thing happened when I arrived and I never heard of this happening again. When the doors of the cattle cars opened, lights shone on us and we heard a voice shouting in German over a loudspeaker. Then – I'll never forget this – this voice announced that there were trucks standing by and whoever couldn't get to a truck would be shot. We all jumped down from the train, running, pushing each other. Everybody wanted to get to those trucks. I couldn't even see the trucks. All of a sudden, some of our people started yelling, "Here they are! Here they are!" The trucks had headlights on and the motors were running. Then the trucks started moving.

Although I was very weak from the two or three days on the train, the typhus and the dysentery, I tried hard. I ran to one truck, but it drove away. I probably could have made it because it wasn't that far away. There was still some room on the truck, but I think it left on purpose. I made my way toward another truck, but I couldn't run anymore; I could only walk. That truck left, too. Again, I think the driver did it on purpose. I didn't make it to any of the trucks and there must have been forty or fifty of them. All the trucks drove away. I thought to myself, "After all the misery I went through in the past two years in the labour camp, this is my end." That was going to be it because I knew by then that the Germans didn't make idle threats.

At that moment I heard dogs barking and saw a lot of bright lights turned on us. The Germans began yelling, "Line up in fives. Line up in fives." With the Germans, it was always five, five, five. Now I saw men with striped uniforms. I tried to ask them questions but the only thing they said was, "Line up, line up. Be quiet, don't say anything. When they ask your age, if one of you is too young, don't tell the truth. If one of you is too old, don't tell the truth." They seemed to be afraid and didn't say anything more. I couldn't understand what they were talking about.

I figured that if they were going to line us up and ask our ages, they weren't planning on shooting us; I started feeling safer. But I was with a few others from the labour camp who began to worry. Maybe they'll shoot us later, I thought. Maybe they're lining us up to shoot us. We had no clue.

This was our first "selection." Although the notorious Josef Mengele was known for doing many of the selections, he didn't do ours that time. Another SS officer did the selection. On command we walked by him and didn't know what he was selecting us for because we didn't know what a selection was. He asked a few people their ages and according to the answer sent them to the right or to the left. We soon learned that one way led to the gas chambers; the other to work. There weren't too many of us who were selected for death in the gas chamber that time because we were all arriving from a labour camp. The old and the weak had already died. We were the strongest ones and that's what they were looking for.

Instead of shooting us, when it got a little bit lighter out they marched us about a kilometre or so right into Birkenau, also known as Auschwitz II. They took us to a big assembly place and told us to take off our clothes. They said we couldn't keep these clothes anymore, but we should make sure to keep our shoes because those were the only shoes we would have. I don't know what happened to my shoes; someone must have taken them. They were bad shoes anyway, already worn out. But somehow I got other shoes. I think I got two of the same foot, but they fit and were better than nothing. Some people had no shoes at all. They then took us for delousing. They shaved all the hair off of our bodies. They disinfected us and then took us to the showers. They gave us striped uniforms. This was the same routine that everyone else went through when they arrived in Auschwitz. Then they lined us up again.

One of the SS officers who was in charge came up to one of the men who was standing in the line and asked him his name. When the fellow answered him, the SS officer clubbed him over the head with his rifle. The man fell down and the officer said, "This is a lesson for you. You don't have a name any more. From now on, you have a number."

I saw the person in front of me put out his arm and a German tattooed a number on his arm. Then it was my turn. I stuck out my arm. I got the number 1 – 4 – 3 – 4 – 2 – 5. From then on, I knew that this was my name. Although I had come from a ghetto and then a labour camp, neither of which were pretty, I had never expected to be branded with a number. Now I really felt that I was a slave. Slavery had begun affecting me from the time I had to put on the Star of David and grew when they closed the ghetto. But a number! It had a terrible impact on me.

The way that Auschwitz-Birkenau functioned had everything to do with the numbers. When we got our striped uniform, we had to write our numbers on a piece of linen. The Germans supplied the ink. We attached these pieces of linen onto a coloured triangle, which they gave us to wear on our uniforms. A red triangle was for political prisoners. According to the Germans, all the Poles who came to Auschwitz were political opponents. A red triangle with a yellow stripe was for Jewish political prisoners – the rest of the Jews wore the two yellow triangles that formed the Jewish star. Then there were dark green triangles worn by criminals – many of them were the kapos, our supervisors. Brown or black triangles were for the Gypsies.

According to these triangles, the Germans and the kapos recognized who we were. Anyone wearing the red inverted triangle over the yellow triangle was considered the dregs of the camp.

Then the Germans put us in what was called "quarantine." I didn't understand what the name quarantine meant. I asked one fellow, but he didn't know either. I think it meant separation. The quarantine area consisted of a whole camp of barracks. It was the gatehouse to hell. That's the only way I can describe it.

A few days after our arrival at Auschwitz, I began to wonder about the incident with the trucks. We had all thought they were going to shoot us for not getting on those trucks. I wondered, then, what happened to the ones who had made it to the trucks? I had spent almost two years with some of those men in the labour camps and many were my friends. Finally I found out what happened to them. Apparently the Germans had played a trick on us, reversing the outcome of what they had announced on the loudspeaker. They took the guys who made it to the trucks right to the gas chambers and they put the rest of us in quarantine in Birkenau. I never heard of that kind of selection occurring again. Clearly, it was just not my time to die.

When I came into the barracks on the first day, I already had enough experience from the labour camp to know how to deal with the living conditions. There were three tiers of bunks. I knew I didn't want to be on the lower bunk because all the dirt and lice fell down from above. If somebody peed in the middle of the night, it went right down onto the person below. I was trying to get either a top or middle bunk, but since the top ones were already taken I went for a middle. Just as I got to the only one that was left, another fellow pushed me away and tried to take it from me. One of the men who was there saw what had happened and spoke up for me, calling out, "Hey, don't push him away. He was there first." The one who pushed me started telling the guy off, but he wouldn't have it. "Don't mouth off to me if you don't want trouble," my new friend warned. His name was Jakob Artman and he became one of my closest friends. He saved my life twice in the next three years and we were devoted to each other until the day he died.

When I settled into the bunk, I thanked my new friend and we started talking. I asked him how long he had been there. He said six or eight weeks and then offered to give me a few tips. For instance, as we were talking I was rubbing my arm where they had tattooed the number. "Don't rub it," he warned me. "It might get infected." When I asked him what Auschwitz was all about, Jakob was straightforward. "It's a very terrible place," he said. "Nobody gets out of here alive." He took me outside the barracks, pointed to a chimney and said, "The only way we're going to get out of this camp is through that chimney."

I could see a huge red brick building but I didn't understand what he meant. When we had arrived in Auschwitz we walked to Birkenau from the railway station and we could smell something burning. Of course, we didn't know there were crematoria in Birkenau. How could any normal human think that in the middle of the twentieth century they were burning human bodies? Those things were too farfetched for us to even think about. But when we came into the quarantine camp, we started wondering what kind of place this was. The kapos would point to the chimney and say, "That's your destination." The ghetto, the labour camps in Poznań... these were all terrible places. Still, there we didn't talk about chimneys, we didn't talk about crematoria, we didn't talk about gas chambers.

Jakob was quick to advise me that I had to be extremely careful in the quarantine camp. He told me that the Germans would try to work me to death there. If I survived, they would just take me to another camp. I told him that I had just come from a labour camp and that Auschwitz couldn't be harder than that. "Oh, yeah?" he replied. Unfortunately, he was right.

Many of us were indeed worked to death in that quarantine camp, with hardly any food. The guards took us out early in the morning and we worked at making roads and digging ditches for the sewers. We were doing all of this because the camp was expanding. There were lots of prisoners, so we didn't have to work fifteen hours a day, but we were doing very hard manual labour. It would have gone much faster if there had been wheelbarrows to take the rocks and move them to where they were supposed to go. But, no, we had to carry them in our hands. The whole thing was designed, I would say, as a test to see if we were able to do this type of work. If we survived three months of the harshness of quarantine, then we qualified to go to the D camp in Birkenau, which was the men's labour camp.

The atrocities that happened in quarantine were horrible. Dr. Mengele was a frequent visitor, although in the beginning we didn't know who he was. He and the officers went through each of the barracks to choose people for all kinds of experiments. We saw men taken away and they never came back. We heard screaming.

Then there was the selection. After I'd been working in the quarantine camp for about two weeks, a kapo came into the barracks and announced that there was going to be a selection, that no Jews would be going to work the next day. The other inmates left and the Jews stayed behind in the barracks. At first I was happy to have a day off work. I was so naive that I didn't know what the selection was for. I thought that maybe the Germans were going to pick the ones who were healthy for special work. To me, we were having a holiday.

Jakob was wiser. He told me that he had heard that people had to be very careful during the selection, advising me to make sure that I knew where my clothes were when I was ordered to undress, to stand up straight, to not ask any questions.

An hour or so later, I saw Dr. Mengele. He came in with his entourage, about half a dozen SS men, and one man in civilian clothes who was taking notes. We had to strip naked. Dr. Mengele sat down and we walked in front of him. He indicated which person should go to the left or to the right. When a person went in one direction, the civilian wrote his number down.

When it was my turn, I saw that the man didn't write down my number. I thought when he took down a number it meant they were going to take that person to another labour camp. Jakob had told me that sometimes, if a person was lucky, the Germans would need him for other work. I thought that I had missed an opportunity. So I went back and I tried to tell him that he had forgotten to write down my number. One of the guards pushed me away. I was almost crying. I was stubborn. I didn't want to stay in Auschwitz. I didn't want to go to the gas chambers. I didn't want to be cremated. I didn't want to die there and I kept pushing back. Finally the guard gave me a good push and I fell over to the other side. I was with the men who didn't have their numbers written down.

Mengele didn't send me to the gas chamber that day. It turned out that it was the inmates whose numbers the civilian wrote down who were doomed. The Germans put them in a special barracks under guard. They didn't get any food or water and they were held there for a couple of days. Then they were put into the gas chamber. That is what I had been begging for. That was how naive we all were when we arrived in Auschwitz. We didn't know anything. The conditions in quarantine were so terrible that I was just desperate to get away from there. At least I was lucky that in the barracks where I was, there were only ordinary selections. Mengele wasn't picking anyone for experiments from our group.

Afterward, I learned more about Josef Mengele. I thought he looked like a movie star, good-looking. He was tall and wore a black SS uniform with shiny boots and I remember the way he walked. I also remember the saying, "You're better off if he doesn't see you." He was one of the doctors in Auschwitz who met the transports coming in, selecting people for work or the gas chambers – sending them right or left. Mengele always selected some people for his experiments; if there were twins among the new arrivals, they were in trouble. I only found out these things about Mengele much later. Thank God I wasn't involved with him very much.

Jakob continued to teach me what to do and what not to do in quarantine. Every piece of advice helped. There were about sixty barracks in the quarantine area. Each barracks consisted of a room that held up to a thousand people, depending on how many inmates the Nazis wanted to squeeze in. There were three tiers of bunks and each bunk could hold six men, but usually it was four or five. When we were sleeping on one side, if one guy rolled over, everybody had to move. It was very cramped. The bunks were plain planks of wood with no blankets whatsoever.

In the centre of the barracks there was a furnace for heat. Firewood went in from one side and a chimney came out the other side, running to the end of the barracks. That was where we sat and ate and socialized. That's where we shared our misery. We sat there until we had to go to bed because when we lay down it was so congested that it was a relief just to fall asleep. We were not supposed to talk after the lights were turned off.

Everything was very strictly supervised by a kapo whose helpers were called foremen. There was talk about Jewish kapos. I was in Auschwitz for two years and I only met two Jewish kapos and a few Jewish foremen. Most of the kapos were ex-prisoners. They had the right to kill us whenever they felt like it. It was lawless. We couldn't complain to anybody and nobody could protect us. I saw people who were killed for nothing – sometimes just talking at night or going to the buckets if they needed to urinate could get someone killed. At night we couldn't go to the washroom after nine-thirty. If we had to urinate at night, we had to do it in our soup bowl or cup. Lots of people, including me, had to pee in their soup bowls because if we did it where we slept, the kapos could kill us right there. Or, if the kapos didn't kill someone, they often crippled him. Jakob warned me not to talk back to the foreman and to do exactly what I was told because the kapos might kill me for no reason at all. That's just the way it was in the barracks.

In each camp in Birkenau, the washrooms were just as big as the barracks and constructed the same, except the washroom had holes to sit on and in the corner, by the door, there were water pipes that ran to the sink. The water ran all the time because it was constantly needed. It wasn't the best water in the world. We drank it, but it was probably contaminated. Sometimes it was blue, sometimes it was brown and sometimes it was yellow. That was the water we washed in. That was the only water we had. We had no choice.

In quarantine, I saw what happened to the people who were selected for the gas chamber. It was a terrifying sight. When we went to work, we couldn't help walking by the barracks where the guards were holding them since it was right at the entrance to the quarantine camp. Even if we walked out of the barracks to go to the washroom, they could see us. If they recognized us, they might call out our names. They knew they were going to die and all they were asking for was water.

One of two brothers that I knew was taken in a selection. The other was in my barracks. I heard him crying at night. When we walked to work the next morning he wanted to see his brother. I don't remember if it was to give him water or not; I think he just wanted to touch his brother or be close to him. The kapos beat him up. I don't know if he died. I never saw him again.

~

One of the first prime ministers of Poland after the war, Józef Cyrankiewicz, wrote in his memoirs that nobody could really know about Auschwitz completely. It was impossible to figure it out. It was a chaotic situation. By the time we grasped what was going on, what could we do to survive? I was already a veteran of camps and misery, but this was something entirely different. This was as if I was on another planet.

Out of necessity, I soon began to figure out my way around. For example, one thing to know was how to hang on to our belongings. We got a bowl for soup and they told us not to lose it. The bowl had a hole in the side with a wire through it and we tied it onto our pants. If we lost our bowl, we had nothing to eat with. We had to sleep with that bowl. We also didn't get utensils. If we already had a spoon but wanted to cut a piece of bread (although the bread we got was so small we didn't need to cut it) we sharpened the edge of the spoon with a stone and that was our spoon and our knife.

We even had to sleep with our shoes on so no one could steal them. If we needed something, we had to trade our bread for it and the only place to do this was in the washroom. That was the one location where we could talk to people privately, and that was where we did business. If we needed a spoon, a sock, a shoe, we could exchange for something else we had. The washroom was the market in Auschwitz.

Birkenau consisted of several camps with roads between them wide enough for a truck or even a tank to pass through. Each camp consisted of fifty or sixty barracks. Quarantine was the first camp. The women's camp was next and then the D camp, which was the main labour camp for all of Auschwitz. There was also a Czech Family Camp and a Gypsy camp.

It was some time in September 1943 when they made the special camp for Czech people from the Theresienstadt camp. The Nazis wanted to get rid of all the inmates from Theresienstadt, but they couldn't do it so freely because it was a well-known camp. It held the intelligentsia of Czech Jews – doctors, scientists and so on – who sent out letters before it was restricted. The world knew about it. So the Germans figured they were going to get rid of them little by little. They sent 15,000 or 25,000 of them at a time to Auschwitz, where they weren't killed right away. Whole families were put in this camp together, which was a novelty. They were given better treatment, decent food and they didn't have to work much, except to clean up the camp. They were allowed to write postcards to send to Theresienstadt and maybe all over the world for propaganda purposes, to show how humane Auschwitz-Birkenau was. In March 1944, about six months after the first arrivals, almost the whole camp was murdered in the gas chambers. The rest were murdered about three months later.

The Gypsy camp contained between 20,000 and 25,000 prisoners. The entire camp was murdered a little bit later than the Czech camp, in the beginning of August 1944, except that what happened with the Gypsy camp was more dramatic. The Czech people hadn't been aware that they were going to be gassed. They went very quietly. They didn't scream and fight for life the way the Gypsies did, because the Gypsies knew what was going to happen to them. There was yelling and shouting the whole day.

Later, as more women arrived, they added another two women's camps. There was also a medical camp and a camp for agriculture. Not far away was another camp called Buna, also known as Auschwitz III. In addition there was a *Magazine*, or warehouse, where the kitchen and the cooks were. The cooks were mostly Soviets who had survived from the time Birkenau was being built in early 1942. The Germans held more than 10,000 Soviet prisoners of war (POWs) in Auschwitz and either worked them to death or killed them in the gas chambers. By the end of the war, less than a hundred had survived.

Then there was a block where the kapos lived. Every camp had a *Lagerkapo,* the main kapo, who was in charge of all the work and the other kapos. The kapos were supervisors of the work details. Each kapo had foremen and so on. It went according to rank.

There was a man in my barracks, five or six bunks away from where my quarters were, who had a bunk to himself. Nobody was above him; nobody was below. At first, I thought maybe I was mistaken. Maybe his bunk-mates were out working or something. This man never went to work. He was never beaten up. He just sat around and was treated a little more humanely than the rest of us. I saw that he had a big knife with a point and a piece of wood that he was whittling. I was always curious. Wherever I was, it was good to know what was going on. That became second nature to me. I asked Jakob if he knew anything about him. How did he get a knife? He clearly had privileges that nobody knew anything about and he didn't talk to anyone. Jakob didn't know much about him but he had heard that he was a German

Jew. He had a red triangle over the yellow one and a yellow stripe on top of that on his uniform.

One day I saw him sitting by the furnace carving some pieces of wood. I went to take a closer look and recognized what he was making – they looked like crude chessmen. Remember, I played chess at school. I was a decent chess player for my age, too, so I was intrigued and asked him if he was a chess player. He just grunted at me, as much as telling me not to bother him. The next day I approached him again and introduced myself. He still didn't tell me his name but did ask if I played chess. Most chess players don't like to brag in case they lose. Decent players don't let on how good they are. I told him that I knew a little bit about the game.

We soon got a little friendlier. He told me that he only needed to make two more pieces and offered to play a game with me sometime. I readily agreed, especially since there was lots of time to kill before the guards shut the lights off at night. He had his own bulb in his bunk, so he could whittle or read. I couldn't understand what this was all about.

About a week later, he called me over. He had a first-rate chessboard. The chess pieces didn't look that good, but at least he had painted them black and white so I could recognize them. We set it up and we played a game. I didn't play very well and after about five minutes he told me that I was a lousy player. I replied that I was doing my best and asked him if he would give me a few tips. "I'm not a teacher," he said, very roughly. We played another game and he gave up, saying, "Nah, you're a lousy player." But he didn't have anyone else to play with, so he called me over again a couple of days later. I went back and he set the board up and we started playing again. He grudgingly admitted that I was playing a little bit better.

After we finished the game, he went to his bunk and took out a piece of cake and offered it to me. Cake, I want you to know, not bread. A piece of bread was like a diamond to me. Can you imagine what cake was? It was a bit stale, but that was the best cake I had ever had in my life. I started to ask him where he got it but he just walked away. I returned to my bunk with the cake. I was in shock. I told Jakob the story and I insisted on giving him some of it. It was the first thing I was able to share with him. I thought we were in heaven. Jakob suggested we eat it somewhere else – he was worried that someone might try to kill me for it.

The days passed by. I went to work on the roads. When I came back to the barracks, the man called me over. We played chess again and he gave me a piece of chocolate, enough to share between two people. When I took it to Jakob, he proposed that instead of eating it, we sell it. We took it to the washroom, where some of the other inmates were, and got a decent piece of bread for it. Only a newcomer who didn't know about hunger would trade bread for chocolate. Another time, the man gave me a cigarette. We were able to get a little trade business going with the things he gave me.

I finally got comfortable enough with my mysterious friend to ask him what his name was and he told me that it was Sigmund. I started to tell him where I came from but he stopped me, saying, "I don't want to know where you come from. I don't want to know about your family. You want to play chess with me, let's leave it at that." We played more and although he was a decent player, I was actually better than he was and it started to show. He was impressed with my playing so we became better friends. Playing chess with him earned me the respect of the entire barracks. Nobody yelled at me anymore.

Once, while we were playing, I lost my queen and Sigmund said, "Make sure you don't lose the queen. That's the most important thing – not only in the game, but in life, too. Don't ever trust a woman. They're smarter than we men are." At that moment I felt that I could ask him more about himself. I asked him why he didn't talk to anyone else and why he was willing to talk to me. He told me that the Gestapo wanted information from him and he was sure that if he talked to someone, they would have no reason to keep him alive. I wasn't going to push him so I left it at that.

About a week after this conversation, there was a strange event that seems hard to believe, but I tell you that I witnessed it with my own eyes. I arrived back at the barracks from work as usual and saw to my surprise that a German soldier was standing at the door and a couple of kapos were blocking the entrance so that nobody could go in. A big black limousine stood right in front of the barracks with a chauffeur at the wheel and a good-looking young officer standing beside the car, smoking a cigarette. I don't know what his rank was, but I could tell that he was a high-ranking officer.

By this time, most of the prisoners from my barracks had arrived from various work details. None of us were allowed in; we all just stood outside, waiting to see what would happen. About half an hour later, the door to the barracks opened and, to our astonishment, a woman walked out. To me, in the middle of Auschwitz, this woman, with her perfume, high-heeled shoes and beautiful clothes, looked like the most beautiful woman in the world. She walked out the door of the barracks, went straight to the car and got in the back with the officer. We all just stood there with our mouths open. It took only a fraction of a minute for the woman to walk to the limousine, but seeing her was like getting an electric shock. They drove away, the German soldier following them on a motorcycle. Then the guards opened the barracks door and we went in.

Everyone else went straight to their bunks, but I went looking for Sigmund. I found him sitting on his bunk with half a dozen packages around him. He called me over and asked me to help him move them into the top bunk. He invited me to sit down and again offered me something to eat. He had never been so nice before. Usually when he gave me something, he handed it over quite roughly. This time he gave me a piece of salami with a piece of bread. I felt as though he was waiting for me to ask a question but I was afraid – he had never wanted to give me any answers before. Finally, he asked, "Don't you want to know who that woman was?" He then told me that the woman I had seen coming out of the barracks was his wife. My first thought was that a man with such a beautiful wife must be very happy. But for someone who was only about forty-five, he looked very haggard. He told me that he was going to tell me some of his story because he liked me and I was a good chess player. "But," he added, "I can't tell you too much – friendship with me might be not good for you."

The last thing I wanted was to lose my food supply and my chess partner. I didn't want to pry too deeply, but here he was, suddenly volunteering information. He told me a very strange story – it sounded like the plot of a movie or novel and to this day I don't know how much of it was true.

Sigmund said that he had been one of the ten richest men in Germany, involved with hotels and some kind of manufacturing. He told me that he had millions of dollars stashed away in a numbered bank account in Switzerland and asked me if I knew what that was. I didn't know what a bank account was, never mind a numbered account. I had never been in a bank. But I just nodded my head; I didn't want to let him know that I was so ignorant.

Sigmund went on to tell me that the Nazis had discovered that he was part Jewish, a *Mischling*, a person of mixed ancestry. He hadn't even known until he was nineteen or twenty years old that his father was Jewish because he had already converted to Christianity before Sigmund was born. His mother wasn't Jewish. But according to Hitler's race laws, because he had two Jewish grandparents, Sigmund was considered a Jew and forbidden from marrying an "Aryan." The Nazis had taken all his factories and hotels and everything he had except for the money. They couldn't get that because he was the only person who knew the number of the Swiss bank account. Sigmund was arrested and taken to Dachau. The main reason, according to him, was that the Nazis wanted to force him to hand over the money in the Swiss bank account. He was afraid that his wife would suffer because she was married to someone considered to be a Jew. He also confided that he had a son who was in the German army and was fighting on the Soviet Front. His son had no idea that he had a Jewish father. He was worried that if he didn't give the Germans what they wanted, his son would not make it out of the army alive.

Sigmund went on to tell me that the SS officer we had seen outside the barracks was his wife's lover – the Nazis were trying to use her to get the Swiss bank-account number. They had brought her to visit Sigmund for exactly that reason, but instead she had begged him not to give her the information they wanted. "If you tell them the number of the bank account," she argued, "they'll kill you. If that happens, I'll kill myself. And they'll kill our son. We're only alive because they want that number."

Sigmund told me that he had already been in a number of different camps and jails – Auschwitz was the last one. If his wife didn't get the information they wanted, he was afraid that the Germans would start torturing him; here the Nazis could do whatever they wanted.

As Sigmund told me his story, he gave me a little bit more food. Then he said that we had to stop fraternizing because it was dangerous for me. When I told Jakob what Sigmund had told me, he didn't believe any of it. I responded that we could at least believe in the chocolate and cake and bread and salami.

A few weeks later, the Germans starting making Sigmund work. He wasn't used to physical labour and he came back half dead. I wanted to help him, but he waved me away. I felt I owed him something, though. I learned a better chess game and got all those treats, making it possible for me and Jakob to do business. I already had better shoes and a pair of socks – hardly anyone had real socks. Most of us just wore pieces of cloth wrapped around our feet.

A day or two later, I tried to speak to Sigmund again. Again he shook his head, warning me that if the Germans thought I knew his secrets, they would come after me. I saw him another few times and he admitted that things were getting worse for him. "They're trying to force me to speak," he told me. "I don't know how long I can hold out."

I never played chess with Sigmund again. He committed suicide.

The camp was surrounded by an electrified wire fence. The current wasn't on all the time, but it was on at night. One night, after the guards had dragged Sigmund back from an interrogation, he left the barracks. He touched the electric wire and was electrocuted. When I came back from work, he was gone. His body had been taken to the crematorium.

The Nazis interrogated me after his death. They didn't torture me, but they questioned me. At the front of the block was what they called in German a *Schreibstube*, which functioned as an administrative office for the commandant of Birkenau and his staff. People from the camp who were fluent in both Polish and German took notes and answered the telephone. They took me down to the office, but I had nothing much to tell them. I told them that I had played chess with the man and that sometimes he gave me something to eat. That was all I knew about him.

∼

One day there was another selection and, after we got dressed, they sent Jakob, me and another few inmates to the D camp. The guards registered us in the *Blockstube*, another administrative office, and spread us around throughout the barracks. I was hoping that Jakob was going to be in the same barracks as me and he was; we always stayed together whenever they marched us in fives. We were sent to Barracks 24.

The living quarters were a little bit better in the D camp. They actually gave us a couple of blankets, one for a cover and one to put over the bare wood. It was a better camp but it was very crowded. Sometimes there were a thousand men in our barracks when a lot more transports arrived, but the average was about eight hundred.

In the D camp, we were just expected to follow the routine. The SS didn't say much about what we did unless someone broke the rules or there was sabotage or one prisoner killed another. For these offences they made the guilty party parade in the front of the barracks and then shot them and sent the bodies to the crematorium. Another punishment was beating. People were clubbed to death, or close to death, for any reason. The kapos tried to show the Nazis that they were worthy of their positions. So if someone lagged behind in a march, they hit him over the head with a stick like a baseball bat. Either they would split his skull or hit him so hard that he fell down. And if he fell down, he was a dirty *Schweinhund* (pig-dog) Jew, daring to lie down on the job. As soon as someone was beaten, he was almost finished.

During the day, nobody remained in the barracks except the people who cleaned them. These men got around the foremen by becoming their lackeys or lovers. I sometimes saw young boys getting food and living well; they didn't have to work. I couldn't understand why. Finally, Jakob explained to me about homosexuals. I had seen these boys leaving the barracks where the kapos lived, so now I knew what they were doing down there.

The very first thing we did when we got up in the morning was run to the washroom and from there to the front of the barracks to be counted by the kapo and the foremen. Nobody could be missing. The kapos had to account for every single person one way or another. If someone was dead or dying, we dragged him out to be counted. Later, he was dragged away to the crematorium. After they counted us we got coffee and a piece of bread as we returned to the barracks. If somebody was missing, we didn't get the coffee and the bread and we couldn't go back to the barracks. We stayed standing out there until the missing person was found. Once we stood there for three days and nights. People were dropping dead – whoever couldn't stand fell down and just lay there. We had to stay like that until the missing person was caught and brought in front of the barracks.

Half an hour after breakfast, they started assembling us for work. Every morning, the *Kommandos,* the work details, were assembled. The kapos could pick and choose and take us any place they wanted. If people had special qualifications or skills, like being carpenters or roofers, the kapos put them in an area for builders. I didn't have any special skills. Jakob was a tailor, but that was nothing special. We nevertheless found out right away that it wasn't healthy to stay in the camp without anything to do. At work people wouldn't get killed unless there was a reason. For the most part, when people died at work it was from exhaustion. It was never a pleasure, but we had fewer problems when we went to work.

Jakob and I found ourselves with another few men who weren't qualified for specific work details. We asked the ones who were more experienced and had been in the camp longer how they got work. They told us that in the morning the kapos picked people randomly for various work details. If we were lucky, we'd be picked for one of the better jobs. Most of the work was in construction. There were certain *Kommandos* that were less desirable than others – ones that were too difficult or where the men had to work out in the cold. I was warned to stay away from these.

Since I didn't have a kapo who I was working for on a steady basis, on the first morning I stood with another few thousand men in an area where the kapos would see us and choose us for work. A few kapos gathered all the stragglers who hadn't been chosen and told us individually where to go, depending on what they needed.

The SS guards mostly stayed at the gates to the camp and they didn't come into the individual camps. At Birkenau, there were approximately a thousand guards, although sometimes there were fewer because the Nazis needed them on the front. When a kapo left the camp with a *Kommando* to go to work, he would tell the SS guard at the gate the number on his arm, plus how many men he was taking. The kapo was responsible for that number of men and he took them to wherever the *Lagerkapo* told him. When the kapo came back with a detail, there had to be exactly the same number of men that he had left with. Even if by then there were five dead and five who'd been crippled, all of them had to be accounted for. The healthy ones had to carry the dead and injured back to the camp with them.

I worked in construction for the first few days. I worked in fields doing all types of back-breaking labour. It was starting to become a routine, but I can't say I liked the work. When I had been in quarantine for a while, we old-timers were able to have it a little bit easier when new transports of men arrived. Because we knew our way around, we had our own little privileges. On the whole it wasn't quite as bad as this new work situation.

It was clear that some *Kommandos* were better than others. When I saw some men trying to get into a particular *Kommando*, I was curious, especially when one day on the way back from work I saw one of them holding his soup bowl in his hand instead of just letting it hang down by a wire on his belt. I passed by him to see why he was holding it that way and I smelled gasoline. Later I saw him coming to the barracks with an extra bowl of soup. I went up to the guy and I said, "Excuse me. I don't want to interrupt you while you're eating." I didn't know if he would talk to me. "Where did you get that soup?"

"From the kitchen, where else?" he said. "There are Russian cooks over there. If you've got some goods you can bargain with them."

He then told me about a big field of broken-up airplanes from various countries. They had been shot down and taken to this field where a work detail dismantled them. The Germans never threw anything away; every part was used. The *Kommando* gathered the parts – wings, motors and so on – which were then loaded onto trucks and taken away. The dismantling was very hard work. The workers didn't have any tools and the Germans didn't care how they did it. The plus side was that sometimes the men who worked there found gasoline. If they could smuggle it into the camp, they would sell it to the Russians for a bowl of soup or some bread. And what did the Russians do with it? They drank it. As far as I could tell, the Russians would drink anything. They drank perfume if they got a bottle of perfume. They drank cologne water and they drank gasoline.

I knew this was a work detail I had been told to avoid by some of the other men. It was terrible work, especially in the cold, and the camp didn't even provide workers with gloves. But I wanted to go there to see if I could get some of this gasoline to trade for extra food. When I got back to the barracks I told Jakob what I had learned and we tried to find out how to join that *Kommando*. The men we asked thought we were crazy, but they told us that if we wanted to be on that work detail we should try to find a kapo by the name of Ziggy, who was always short of people for his crew.

The next day, we made sure we were in front of the line for that detail. Ziggy couldn't understand why we would volunteer. Usually the kapo had to yell, "Come on, come on" for people to join. And when a kapo said, "Come on," you knew you'd better go. Ziggy took us and we worked and worked. At first we didn't find anything. Then, after two or three days, I noticed that some guys were trying to get to the top of the airplanes, where the motors were. This seemed strange to me. The motors gave off a terrible smell and going near them was dangerous. Sometimes the planes still carried live ammunition that could explode or catch fire. But that was where the gasoline was and there were quite a few men searching for it. In reality, there were not that many tanks of gas that we could find anyway. What's more, by the time we found them, how many still had gasoline in them? I managed to get to a tank, but I couldn't siphon off the gasoline because the tank was mounted. I called Jakob to help me, but he was worried that we could get shot for that. I replied that we could get shot for lots of things. He came and helped me and we siphoned off whatever gasoline we could. Jakob was always like that. I was too reckless but he would always help me.

I put the gasoline in my soup bowl, but as I was going back to the barracks, I spilled a little because my fingers were frozen. We passed the gate to get back into the camp. If the German guards had seen us, I don't know what they would have done; they would definitely have thought it was odd for us to be entering the camp holding our bowls in our hands. But there was no other way to do it and I somehow got my gasoline into the camp.

By then I had only a few drops left in the bowl and wondered if I had enough to trade. I figured that whatever the case, at least it would give me a chance to find out how to do business. Somehow I had to get to the kitchen to do the trade, but the kitchen was strictly off-limits. There was no one around to really guide me and tell me how to go about doing this. Only a close friend like Jakob would have been able to teach me how to get to the kitchen and he didn't know either.

The first time I tried to sneak to the kitchen a kapo caught me and demanded to know what I was doing there. "I'm looking for something," I said. He probably knew what I was up to. He smacked me over the head, but not too hard. I lost the little bit of gasoline that I had and ran away. I was lucky. He could have done more damage. Maybe he was in a good mood.

I wondered how I would manage to get the gasoline to the kitchen without losing it or getting smacked around first. But I didn't give up. One time, when I came back from work with a nice amount of gasoline, a couple of other men attacked me and took the bowl away. I saw a kapo coming and noticed that they were in cahoots. By that time I was enough of a veteran to know not to ask questions.

Finally, I established contact with a Russian cook. When I gave him the gasoline, I had to trust that he was going to give me some soup. He knew why I had brought him the gasoline. He transferred it into his own bowl and said to me, "Tomorrow." So the next day I had to wait around near the kitchen, exposed and in danger of being beaten up, hoping that this guy would be honest enough to give me something. He did indeed come and he gave me a bowl of soup. Now I had an extra bowl. I took the soup and ran back to the barracks, where I shared it with Jakob. The bowl alone was worth a piece of bread since so many people, by the time they came in and learned the ropes, had lost their bowls or had them stolen. No one could get soup without a soup bowl, so I had something to sell. I went to the market in the washroom. I don't remember what I got for the bowl but I think it was a pair of socks. I was hoping for a pair of socks. Mine were already worn out and I had to put paper in my shoes to keep my feet warm. The old-timers taught us that trick.

I had quite a bit of luck. Soon I had about six Russian customers. One of them would meet me right away with a bowl of soup. These men knew that guys like us were going to come around to make a trade – it wasn't like we had to knock at their doors. Naturally they were afraid too since there was a guard watching them in the kitchen, but they wanted the gasoline so they managed somehow. These Russian cooks were long-time survivors and they knew what they were doing. They already had food and could eat whatever they wanted. They ate all the fat that we were supposed to get in the soup. But they wanted cigarettes, perfume and gasoline. We had gasoline but wanted food. It worked both ways.

My new trade business went on for a little while. Every time I got a bowl of soup, I made a further exchange. Sometimes I got socks or extra underwear. Sometimes I even traded for a cigarette and for this cigarette I could buy a piece of bread. There were smokers for whom a cigarette was more important than bread.

I never got caught during the time I worked in the airplane field looking for gasoline. There were no SS around. There were only foremen and kapos and there were too many people working there for them to watch all of us. If we carried our soup bowls in our hands, it was very hard to tell if it was because we couldn't tie the bowls to our pants or if we were carrying something in them. Some people, for instance, carried water in their bowls. Ziggy, the kapo, saw us holding our bowls and didn't say anything. I said to myself, "We have a good kapo. How come he doesn't say anything?" Then when I went by him one time, I saw that he had a yellow stripe. He was a Jew – the only Jewish kapo I ever worked for.

As I learned later, Ziggy was a German Jew, one of the refugees from the ill-fated 1939 voyage of the SS *St. Louis*, also known as the "Voyage of the Damned." I don't know what happened to the rest of the passengers. Maybe there were others in Auschwitz, but I only met him. The Nazis needed him because his language skills were perfect. As long as they needed him, they kept him alive. He had been a professional before the war, something like an engineer or teacher, so they made him the kapo of this airplane detail. I'm certain he figured that if we wanted to smuggle gasoline, we should help ourselves.

This *Kommando*, however, didn't last long and soon the salvaging work at the field diminished. After two or three months, the work detail was dissolved and I was looking for work again. Where I worked and what I had to do were extremely important. It was crucial that the work didn't kill me and that I could join a *Kommando* with a kapo or foreman who wasn't too cruel or bloodthirsty. I decided to ask Ziggy for his help.

I had heard that there was a good kapo whose detail was assigned to work on the electric fence. I went up to Ziggy one morning and asked if he knew of a decent kapo, like him, to work with. He could keep me in his *Kommando* if he wanted to and he could even force me to work for him, but he already had lots of workers. I told him that the hard work details were getting to me and I wanted to survive. I shouldn't have said I didn't want hard work because he might have thought I was lazy. I had to be careful. I told Ziggy that I had heard about a *Kommando* that worked at the electric wires and wondered if he could help me. He seemed to recognize me, or maybe he saw how young I was. He took pity on me and advised me to look for kapo Manfred. I thanked him and then saluted him. I didn't want to shake hands with him. The Nazis were like kings and the kapos were the princes.

The Neutral Zone

It took me about three days to find kapo Manfred. Meanwhile, I had to work in other horrible places because I was a newcomer and I was always getting the short end of the stick. For instance, if one guy had to take three bricks, I had to take ten. I also had to carry cement and take shingles up to roofs, which was gruelling work. When I finally found kapo Manfred, I did my best to speak to him very nicely, asking him if I could work for his detail. He in turn asked me what I knew about electricity. I answered, "All I know about electricity is that you can electrocute yourself." Kapo Manfred laughed and told me to report to him the next morning. I saw right away he was not the kind of kapo who, when I asked him something, would clobber me.

The next day I got up early and ran to make sure that I found kapo Manfred. He was assembling about a hundred people. The group was then split into smaller groups of twenty-five and he took me in one. His work was very interesting and probably saved my life.

His *Kommando* was called the "Neutral Zone." Each camp was surrounded by its own electric wire fence; then there was the main fence that surrounded Auschwitz. Between the two was a narrow asphalt road, somewhat like a sidewalk, for the electricians to use when they had to fix the wires. Along the road ran a wire, about a metre high, on posts. The Neutral Zone lay between the road and this little wire. In the winter we cleared it of snow and ice. In the summer we had to clear it of weeds and grass or anything else that would touch the wire and short out the electricity. We often found dead bodies hanging on the wires – suicides were frequent. When a body was on the electric wire, it broke the current. If we found a body hanging on the wire, we removed it and put it aside. There was a special *Kommando* of people who gathered the bodies and wheeled them to the crematoria on a cart to dispose of them.

We were provided with tools and a wheelbarrow. Nobody bothered us. Nobody yelled at us. Once I had had a few days to get to know the men I was working with, I asked them about Manfred. One of the fellows had found out that Manfred was a German communist who had been arrested when the Reichstag was burned in 1933. I didn't know much about the politics in Germany, but he explained that they arrested many communists and ex-communists then, accusing them of trying to overthrow the government. If the Nazis wanted to arrest someone, they simply said he was a communist. Manfred, however, really was a communist. He had been in Dachau and several other concentration camps before they sent him to Auschwitz, where he became a kapo. "He is like an angel," the fellow assured me. Manfred was a very humane, decent man, which was rare to find in Auschwitz. We were very lucky. Everybody wanted to work with Manfred.

Since I was the newcomer I was assigned to work with a professional electrician. I dug holes for new posts, mixed concrete, poured it in the holes and placed the posts with the electric outlets into the concrete. If there weren't enough posts or material, I had to clear the weeds around the Neutral Zone. A watchman patrolled the area and every time he came by we saluted him. He already knew who we were and didn't bother us. Naturally, we didn't bother him either.

Occasionally we worked near the women's camp. Sometimes the women would call out to us and we called back. We even joked around with them. Things were going relatively smoothly until sometime in the spring of 1944, when big transports started arriving from

Hungary. Transports came in one after another in 1944. It was the busiest time in Auschwitz. Obviously, nobody told us anything. We just saw lots of people arriving and later, when the men came to our barracks, we learned that they were from Hungary. Some of them spoke Yiddish, but they mostly spoke Hungarian and a little bit of German. They told us stories and they asked us questions. We told them what we knew.

During this time, we saw that the crematoria were belching out more smoke than usual. Up until this point, I hadn't been far out enough to see that there were four crematoria. But one day I went down another road and saw a plain, ordinary farmhouse with people working around it. They called the area the "ditches."

The very first gas chamber at Auschwitz was in this farmhouse. When they decided to gas people before the more modern crematoria, which also contained gas chambers, were built, they did it there. They made one big room inside the house, sealed it up and converted it into a makeshift gas chamber. Maybe it wasn't that efficient but what did they care if the Jews were going to suffer another five or ten minutes. They dug deep ditches, put wood in them, lit fires and threw the bodies in. Human bodies were burning all the time and the air was full of smoke and stink. There was a special *Kommando,* called the *Sonderkommando,* who worked in the gas chambers. They were Jewish prisoners from the camp who had to drag the bodies out of the farmhouse and take them to be burned. These people also had to cut the victims' hair to be used in mattresses and check the dead bodies for gold fillings.

When the new crematoria were built, they had stopped using the ditches. I didn't even know they existed until the Hungarian transports started arriving so frequently that they needed more room. The crematoria didn't have the capacity for so many people so the Nazis started using the ditches again.

A fiend named Josef Ekhardt became the commander of the ditches in 1944 and oversaw the people who worked there. He was an officer who had been wounded on the Soviet Front and the Germans gave special positions in Auschwitz to soldiers who had been wounded. They received privileges like alcohol and women and they didn't have to work as hard. They could help themselves to the treasures taken from the transports, even gold teeth from the dead bodies. They became big shots. Auschwitz was a world of its own.

The farmhouse was in an open field and it wasn't enclosed with electric wire. Kapo Manfred got the order from the *Schreibstube* to start putting the posts in for the electricity and I was charged with digging holes for the posts. A few days after we started working there, we saw a transport arrive at the camp. Instead of going through a selection, the SS shipped them directly from the station to the ditches. I could see them about 150 metres from us, sitting, waiting to go into this farmhouse. They didn't know what was going to happen to them. We saw the SS standing by with dogs and machine guns. We weren't supposed to see this. We were so close that suddenly the SS who were in charge of the transport spotted us. A soldier on a motorcycle roared up and yelled, "What are you guys doing here? Who gave you the right to be here?"

Maybe kapo Manfred didn't realize that we were too close, or maybe it just happened by accident. Most of the time we worked inside the fence. Here we were on the outside. Whenever we were outside, there were always guards around. The SS officer ordered us to go back into the camp. "Don't come back," he warned us. He had a gun in his hands. Maybe he thought we were trying to escape. We went back quickly and told Manfred what had happened. At the same time the SS men probably got in touch with the camp commander, too. He gave shit to Manfred for sending us there.

Manfred told his foreman to only take us back there to finish the work when there were no transports. A few days later we went back and we started working, putting in the posts. But soon enough, another transport arrived. This time we were on the inside of the perimeter of the camp, so we weren't exposed. We saw more people joining that transport and then we heard screaming and yelling. When we came back the next day, we saw that everyone in the transport had been shot dead.

The modern crematoria were very different from the farmhouse. When people walked into the buildings, they didn't know they were going to a gas chamber. The facilities were cleaned and fumigated. There were even phony showers. The SS told the victims, "Make sure you remember where you put your clothes." They wanted everything to be clean and nicely done. That way it would go quickly and there would be no problems. By the time the people found out what was going to happen to them, they were inside, where gas came out of specially designed gas columns.

Every crematorium had a German SS commander and maybe a half a dozen engineers. The *Sonderkommando* workers, about 1,000 or 1,200 people, were often murdered in special selections and then replaced with new workers. The Nazis didn't want to keep some of them too long in case they got organized to rebel. Everything ran smoothly that way.

At the ditches, however, there was a problem. Josef Ekhardt, the commander, was especially monstrous. What he was doing to the young people before they went to the gas chamber was so atrocious that we could hear them screaming from miles away. I don't know exactly what kind of brutality it was. He didn't care if the killing went smoothly or not. He didn't care if there were still bodies lying around, just as long as he could pack more in.

The maximum number of bodies that could go in the ditch at one time was about two hundred or so. When it was already full, if there were a few children left over, the SS threw them alive on top of the two hundred. And because they could only kill two hundred people at a time and there were a few thousand of them, it took a few days. Because the Hungarian transports came so often and so quickly, when the last people came in, they could see what was going on. Can anyone imagine what these people went through, waiting to be gassed? I don't think anybody can imagine a hell like this. They started rioting, screaming and yelling.

The day we were there, Josef Ekhardt apparently gave an order to the SS who accompanied the transport to kill everyone with machine guns. Maybe there were about a thousand or two thousand people there. It's hard to tell. I just have to guess. But we saw this: we saw these people waiting at the farmhouse one day. The next day, about a mile away, all of them were lying dead. So we knew what happened.

It took some time for the other Nazi big shots to find out what happened there because they were so busy with the transports. At that time, the main person in charge at Auschwitz was the commander Rudolf Höss, and SS-Hauptscharführer (squad leader) Otto Moll was in charge of the crematoria. Someone overheard that Moll reprimanded Ekhardt for overdoing it. One person told another. Rumours, hearsay. But Colonel Moll was supposedly a very ruthless man himself, so it was really something for him to tell Ekhardt to tone down what he was doing. Or maybe it was just because it wasn't done quietly. In the end the *Sonderkommando* went in with wheelbarrows and trucks. They took the bodies to the crematoria and everything was cleaned up in maybe three days.

~

In the fall of 1943, around the time that I first came to Auschwitz, something happened that had a big impact on me. It changed my life and the lives of many inmates in Auschwitz. I didn't witness it but I did hear about it.

There was a rumour going around about the first heroine in Auschwitz. In October 1943, a very famous, beautiful Jewish actress from Warsaw came in a transport with her two children. When it came time to go to the gas chamber, she was undressing and an SS guard – who turned out to be named Josef Schillinger – marched up to her. From what people told me, he made some kind of remark that there was going to be a beautiful soap made from her.

Maybe she knew what was happening because in Warsaw, by then, they had already heard stories of the mass murders. Apparently she said, "Why don't you come closer and help me undress?" He was supposedly very infatuated with her. He came closer and she grabbed his pistol and shot him and another SS guard named Emmerich. Schillinger died. A few seconds later, she was mowed down by machine gunfire. Because there was chaos and the Germans didn't know who did what they shot everybody there, too – a few hundred people. They just killed everyone, which was a blessing for those people anyway. Better to die by a bullet than the gas chamber.

The story gave people a big boost. This was the first time they had heard of a woman doing something like this and she became a sort of mythic figure, a heroine. People idolized her. There was an underground Polish resistance movement operating in Auschwitz with links to the Polish Home Army and when they found out what happened, from what I heard, they became ashamed that they hadn't done enough. It took a Jewish woman grabbing a revolver and shooting an SS man to show that the SS weren't invincible.

There was a *Kommando* that was called Kanada where Jakob got work, probably because he was a tailor. The people in this *Kommando* sorted the shoes, clothes and other goods from the transports. They disinfected the items, put them together and packed them up to send to Germany. A few thousand people worked there. One department worked with hair, one worked with inspecting the clothing for hidden valuables, one worked with the shoes and so on. They were searched after work, but if they could steal something, they took it back to the barracks to sell. The Underground had told the people in Kanada to try to find out who the actress was. There were belongings of hundreds of thousands of people there and they had to sort through them all, so this took a little bit of time. But they found photographs of her when they were sorting her clothes and possessions and the people who were involved in the Underground stashed them away in their barracks. Whoever had a chance, went to see them. Those photographs became like a shrine. Nobody told me her name. Maybe somebody knew it, but nobody mentioned it. We could have been killed just for having a photograph.

Jakob was the one who told me this story. Because he was working in Kanada, he knew about the search for her photographs. A Jewish woman, who I later learned was the big star Franceska Mann, had become a legend to us. I had the privilege of seeing the photos once and I saw a beautiful woman in black and white. Jakob wasn't really sure that this was the photograph of the same woman, but I was inspired when I looked at this woman's picture. How could a Jewish woman do this? People were saying after the war that Jews were going like sheep to the gas chamber. It wasn't so easy. What did we know about gas chambers? What did we know about fighting? We didn't have any leaders.

Many years later, I saw the film *Funny Girl*. That was the first time I saw Barbara Streisand. I reacted strangely and broke out into a sweat because her face was so like the one I remembered in the photograph. I could not believe it. To me, that was my image of the actress who had inspired the Underground at Auschwitz. Now every time a movie with Barbara Streisand is playing, I tell my wife that I want to see it.

～

Still more Hungarian Jews arrived at Auschwitz. One day, while I was working for kapo Manfred, I was assigned to clean up near the women's camp. A woman came along and yelled out to me in Hungarian. I motioned to her that I didn't know the language. She spoke broken Yiddish and broken German and managed to ask me which barracks I came from. I told her I was from barracks 24. She then asked if I knew her husband and gave me his name. She wanted me, if I had a chance, to call out his name to see if he was there. I agreed just to get rid of her. She didn't realize that I couldn't just go in the barracks yelling out a name. I motioned to her to leave since she could be shot from the watchtower. When I went back to the barracks, however,

I called out the name just to see if this guy was there. Nobody answered. I went among the Hungarian men because the groups that came from each country liked to stick together. I called out the name again. Again, nobody answered me. Fine, I figured. It was better this way. I didn't want to be involved.

About three days later, when I went back to finish the work, this woman came out and called to me again. I motioned "no" to her, but she was stubborn. I yelled out to her, "Don't come near here!" The guard, after all, didn't need the excuse of waiting until she came close to the Neutral Zone to shoot at her – the guards shot lots of people just for their own amusement. "I don't care," she said. "I want to know if my husband's alive. I want him to know I'm alive." She took out a small rock with a piece of paper tied to it on which she had written her husband's name, her name and a word in Hungarian that probably meant "alive." How much could she write on a scrap of paper? She already knew which barracks he was in. I don't know how she found out. She threw the rock over to me. I figured that I might as well take it. She was risking her life.

I grabbed the rock, put it inside my uniform and smuggled it back to the barracks. I asked a few Hungarian men, "Do you know a man by this name? He's supposed to be in this barracks." One fellow answered that he knew a man with that name in another barracks. I had a little bit of a conscience. I saw a woman who wanted to know about her husband, so I thought I may as well try to help. I went to the other barracks and called out the name and a man answered. I called him over. He said to me, in broken Yiddish, "Are you looking for me?" I told him that I had a letter from his wife and gave him the piece of paper with the rock because I wanted to show him how I got it. I didn't want him to think I could just do this easily. They were newcomers. They knew as little as I did when I first arrived. He started shaking my hand and he spoke to me in Hungarian. I told him that I didn't understand – I already knew enough in Hungarian to say, "I don't understand." He kissed the piece of paper and started hugging me,

saying, "Oh, thank you, thank you. I didn't know my wife was alive."
They were young people, maybe in their thirties. He was so happy
that he started crying. The man then asked me if I could give her a
message. I told him that I couldn't carry any more messages, but how
could I say no? I told him I would do it once, but not to ask me again.
He wrote a note and wrapped it around the rock. I warned him that I
didn't know where I would work tomorrow but he begged me to take
it with me in case I got the chance to give it to her.

It wasn't easy to carry the rock around. We didn't have any pockets. They made our uniforms without pockets so that we couldn't
carry any weapons. I was working somewhere else for two days but I
somehow managed to carry the rock with me. But how long could I
carry it? I was afraid. I went to one of the foremen and I asked him to
get me an assignment near the women's camp. There was a hierarchy,
so the foreman usually had to ask the kapo for me. He said he would
try and the next day he arranged it. Some of these guys weren't so
bad, but you had to know which ones they were.

I went back to work around the fence near the women's camp.
This poor woman had been waiting two days for me. When she saw
me she waved so I would recognize her. Believe me, the women in
the camps weren't easy to recognize. All of them were emaciated; they
hardly looked like women at all. A man without hair who dressed like
this didn't look so bad, but for a woman, it was terrible. I threw the
rock over to her. I didn't know that this one throw was the beginning
of my next new career, so to speak. I threw the rock and went back to
my regular routine.

That night, I had about half a dozen Hungarians coming to my
bunk. There I was, having my soup and minding my own business
and these men asked if I would throw a message to their wives. Each
one of them was holding a rock in his hand with a paper wrapped
around it and, lo and behold, a piece of bread. I was in business.

The first man had told his friends what happened. And the wife
told her friends that there was a means of communication. I didn't

know what to do, but I knew what it meant in terms of getting extra food. So I took the rocks and I tried to explain to them that this was dangerous and I could not be sure that I would find their wives. Some of them understood a little bit of Yiddish. Polish Jews could speak Yiddish, but not all Hungarian Jews and when they did, it was not too good. But they understood what I was talking about. They still wanted me to try.

The next day, I carefully hid the rocks between the folds of my tucked-in shirt and pants and I threw them over to the women. The women grabbed the stones and hurried away. When I came back to the barracks, I had more customers and more pieces of bread. I suppose I could make myself out as a hero, telling you that I was a nice guy and I said, "Okay, guys, give me the rocks. I'm going to give your wife or your kids information. I don't want your bread." No, I wasn't that dim-witted. I don't think any human being can really understand the pain of hunger if he has never experienced it. This is something you cannot imagine. You can break a leg and then if your friend breaks a leg you know how he feels. But how many people know about starvation?

I had been hungry ever since the ghetto and it never stopped. I'd seen people kill each other for a piece of bread. I saw a father and a son fighting for a piece of bread. I saw it with my own eyes. So I'm not going to be a hypocrite and tell you that I didn't take a piece of bread when I could. I'm not going to pretend that I didn't do business when somebody offered me a piece of bread that I could eat or trade.

At first the foreman didn't notice what I was doing, but sooner or later he caught me throwing a rock and warned me that I would get everyone into trouble. I could get shot and everyone would be punished. I figured that I could bribe him and maybe keep the business going. I promised him that I wouldn't do it anymore and gave him a piece of bread. He still told kapo Manfred because he knew something bad was going to come out of it. He was afraid and he was right to be afraid. He was already a veteran. Manfred called me over and told me that he wanted me to stop because if I was caught the whole group would be shot. He said that he would give me one more chance but either I had to stop throwing the rocks or I couldn't work for him anymore. I promised him that I wouldn't do it again. But I did do it one more time.

On that day, a woman came around and threw a rock to me. She said, "For my son," in Yiddish. I thought of my mother, which convinced me to help out just this one last time. The woman told me which barracks her son was in. I never could understand how they knew that. I found the son and gave the message to him. He was so happy that his mother was alive. Right away he wrote out another note and gave it to me. He spoke a little Yiddish so I told him that I couldn't do it. I explained that I had only given him the note because if my mother was able to contact me, I would be happy too.

I was almost twenty years old. He was probably fifteen or sixteen. He went down on his knees, holding out all the bread that he had for the day and said, "I want my mother to know that I'm alive." He really got to me. He was crying. I didn't have any tears left to cry for my mother, but I knew how he felt. So I reluctantly agreed. I took the rock and I said, "I don't want your bread. I don't want to be in this business. I'll do it once more for you but tell your friends that I'm not going to do it again." He shoved the bread into my hands. He knew if I took his bread, I was going to take the rock. I gave half of the bread back to him.

I threw the stone back to his mother but that was it for my new adventure in business. When I came back from work, before my foreman could report me, I told kapo Manfred, "I've done it one last time. I had to do it, kapo. If you want to fire me, okay." But he happened to be a very fine man. It's too bad that I know nothing more about him, whether he survived or not. I just knew his name, Manfred. Go look up a Manfred, right?

I told everybody I wouldn't throw any rocks again and I didn't. I didn't want to endanger the kapo and the other men. The Germans could dispose of the whole *Kommando* if they saw any monkey business going on. There was no shortage of labourers.

~

I thought my smuggling business was finished but it turned out that, because of the Underground, it wasn't. I didn't know very much about the Underground before because I only joined them after the rock-throwing incidents. They somehow found out that I was brave enough to throw stones for people and they were always looking for somebody crazy and brave like I was. I learned that some members of the Underground had belonged to the Polish Home Army in Warsaw and the two organizations co-operated. The Underground was in communication with the Polish Home Army, which had assisted in several uprisings, including the Warsaw Ghetto Uprising in April and May 1943. There were very few Jews in the Underground. Even in Auschwitz, the Poles didn't like the Jews. If these men in the Underground gave you an order, you had to carry it out. If you didn't carry it out, they'd kill you themselves.

One evening after the episode with the rocks, two men came into my barracks. I'd never seen them before, but I could tell they were Poles. They were big, strong men. One of them told me they wanted to talk to me in the washroom. "We have something for sale," the Polish man said. This was common, so no one in my barracks was suspicious. I had nothing to buy or sell, but I went with them, thinking, "What the hell do they want from me?" One of the men said, "Let's go slowly. We just want to talk to you." He then explained that they needed me to do them a favour. They wanted me to throw a few stones over a fence. I told them that I couldn't throw any more stones because I had already gotten in trouble over that. Besides, kapo Manfred would kill me himself if I took that risk again. The Pole said that he was already ahead of me on that one. He had spoken to kapo Manfred, who knew about their request. The Pole then gave me a spiel about how important he was. I knew that there was a political hierarchy among the Poles in the camp. A lot of them were there for political reasons or for sabotage. I asked them why I should do it for them and they answered, "Because we are ordering you to." They then gave me a rock with a piece of paper. I don't know what was on it, of course.

The next morning, the first thing I did was go to the foreman and tell him that I wanted to talk to the kapo. Manfred wasn't the kind of a kapo who had to show the SS that he was lord and master over our lives. I went up to him and very politely asked if I could talk to him. Sometimes we had to take our hats off, too. If a German passed by and we didn't snap our hats off, he might shoot us right on the spot. A kapo, if we didn't take our hats off smartly, could hit us too. But when I tried to take off my hat, Manfred insisted that I didn't have to.

We went to the tool shed for privacy and Manfred told me that the two men had been to see him. I asked him why he allowed them to use me for delivering the rocks. I told him that I didn't want to do it. That's when Manfred told me about the Polish Underground at Auschwitz. "You don't dare say no to them," he explained. "I don't want anything to do with them but I have to carry out their orders because I know some black night they can cut my throat. They said they needed you so I said okay." I didn't know how powerful the Underground was. Manfred told me to do whatever they told me to and to keep him informed. "Maybe you'll do it once or twice," he said, "and then they won't need you anymore and you can forget about it."

I think that I threw this first rock to the hospital camp. Two days later I had another contact with them and another rock to throw to another camp. Because an electric wire fence separated the camps from each other and some camps were separated by roads for trucks and cars as well, sometimes the rock throwing was harder. My next assignment was when I was near the Czech Family Camp. I remember this vividly because I did not throw the rock to a person. Maybe someone was supposed to arrive later, or maybe they didn't trust me, or maybe that person just wasn't able to come. I couldn't tell with the

Underground. They only told me what they wanted to tell me. They gave me rocks to throw and said, "Throw as hard as you can." Perhaps it was just a test to see if I could throw, or if I would do it. I don't even know if there was anything on the paper. Sometimes I don't think so. And that was it for a little while.

It was sometime in April, a few weeks, or maybe a month after the rock-throwing, that I was called by the main kapo on the loud-speaker to report to the SS. I can recall the month precisely now be-cause some sixty-five years later, while I was visiting Auschwitz, the archivist there presented me with the log book with my name and the date I was arrested.

When I reported to the office, two SS men brought me into an interrogation room where, after getting past the formalities of who I was and where I was born, a senior officer asked me what business I had regarding throwing stones from the neutral zone to the women's barracks. I was in shock. I must have been seen by one of the guards in the towers and I guess it had taken some time for them to iden-tify me and bring me in for questioning. I told him the truth. I told them that it was nothing, just a Hungarian woman throwing a stone through the fence to me for her husband and that I had thrown one back later. It was weeks ago and I told him I hadn't done it again.

I don't think it mattered what I said, but then again, they could have just shot me on the spot. Instead, the two SS men took me to the penal barrack, "the penal colony" as we prisoners called it. This was a barrack for the prisoners who had done something wrong, but not something punishable by death. I was put on very tough work details involving heavy physical labour. Mostly the work entailed clearing woods and rocks to prepare for special equipment to build roads outside of the camp in what later became called the Mexiko camp. Sometimes the work involved cleaning up around the train landing after a transport. It was difficult and I didn't think I could survive the work for long, but then two or three days after being transferred there, the barrack commander gave me a new job. I was to stay back and help clean the barracks, bring the food from the kitchen and clean up the barrack commander's office. I couldn't believe my luck; this was the best work possible. I realized later that someone from the Underground must have arranged it. They had the influence and no one else would have cared. In any case, about three or four weeks later I was transferred back to my regular barrack, number 24, not much worse for wear.

Some time passed and then one day, someone approached me from the Underground with a special assignment. They wanted me to get onto a *Kommando* going to Buna, one of the subcamps of Auschwitz and, once there, to talk to a young Jewish engineer from Italy named Primo who knew very little German. The Underground's "runners" – people who worked for them – had already tried to talk to him without any luck. Now I was to be a runner for them too. The other runners hadn't been able to communicate with him because he only spoke French, Italian and very broken German. The Poles didn't speak German the way Jews spoke it. We spoke better German because Yiddish is so similar to German. I told them that I would do it but they would have to ask my kapo first. They said that they had already spoken to my kapo and arranged things so that wherever they needed me, they didn't have to ask for permission. Kapo Manfred was really afraid of them. I found out later how truly powerful they were.

They soon arranged to send me with a *Kommando* to Buna. The Buna factory works, which were very large, mostly made synthetic oil and rubber. Many companies were built in and around Auschwitz; they were located there because the area was not a bomb target and there was a huge supply of labour. There were close to 15,000 people incarcerated in Buna. Elie Wiesel, the famous writer, was one of them. Every day, a *Kommando* from Birkenau walked over to Buna to work on specific projects. These guys were picked to do precision work and to dig ditches for pipes and poles. The kapo who took us there was none other than Ziggy. The Underground needed a kapo whom they could depend on. Ziggy knew that he was supposed to take me with him when he was assembling the *Kommando* that morning. I'm quite sure Ziggy was either a member of the Underground or that he took orders from the Underground.

Buna was built very close to a little town called Monowitz, where there was a British POW camp that few people knew about. More than a thousand British POWs were imprisoned there from the fall of 1943 until the beginning of 1944, when hundreds were transferred, leaving the camp population at about six hundred. POWs weren't supposed to do any direct war-related labour, but these British POWs weren't sitting idle. The Germans still forced them to work and they were always up to something. When the Underground found out about them, they got in touch. I cannot tell you how. I don't know. I was only a little pawn in their game.

One of these POWs was a man by the name of Charles Coward, who was later named as one of the Righteous Among the Nations by Yad Vashem in Jerusalem, together with men like Oskar Schindler and Raoul Wallenberg. He had been taken prisoner by the Germans at Dunkirk and had made several attempts to escape. At the Monowitz POW camp, which was close enough to Buna to witness how Jewish prisoners were treated, he started bribing the guards around him for information and soon he knew what was happening in Auschwitz and he tried to do something about it.

Charles Coward was known as "the Count of Auschwitz." I didn't find out his real name until many years later. The Underground called him the Baron for short. He had more freedom to move around from place to place, both inside and out of the camp, and could contact the workers inside the factories, because he was the Red Cross liaison. Although there was always a German guard accompanying the POWs, they could bribe the guards who had already smartened up a little – most knew the war was not going to last much longer. The Germans had already lost Stalingrad more than a year ago. The POWs got packages with chocolate and cigarettes from home and from the Red Cross, things that the Germans didn't have, so they were easily bribed.

A few hundred Italian and French Jews worked at the factories in Buna. Some of them were engineers and one of the engineers was so clever that he worked inside a factory helping with the machinery. This was Primo, who I was supposed to get in touch with. Years later, when I heard about the author Primo Levi, I thought it might have been him, but the man I met in Auschwitz was an Italian engineer, not a chemist as Primo Levi was. The Underground needed someone to go inside the building when the guards weren't looking and to make contact with the British P O W s, and they wanted Primo's help with this.

As I said, I learned that the Polish Home Army and the Underground in Auschwitz were in communication, and somehow the Polish Home Army found out that Charles Coward was in Auschwitz. The Underground was able to get in touch with him through runners like me. That is why they needed people who were not afraid of going between Buna and Birkenau to carry packages to the Underground. They needed people like me and another few fellows who didn't know each other.

As far as I understood, the way the system worked was that the Baron would go into the factory and find a way to slip a package to a worker from Birkenau. This was very, very dangerous because there were so many people who might see and there were guards armed with guns. Sometimes the Baron didn't have a chance to pass the package directly to a runner, so they tried to find another way to transfer it. This is where Primo came in: they needed somebody who worked inside the buildings and could receive the package from the Baron where nobody could see the exchange. Sometimes people from our *Kommando* helped carry heavy machinery or cement sacks inside and then an inside worker, such as Primo, would slip the package to one of us runners.

Primo caught the eye of the Underground. He was a very intelligent young man and, being Jewish, they figured he would help. I was supposed to find him, so the first time I went out with Ziggy to Buna a member of the Underground pointed Primo out to me. I was digging ditches outside the factories for electric wires and sewers. I wasn't too happy about this because it was hard work and I was afraid of losing my usual position with kapo Manfred, but the Underground said I only had to go a few times. Now I had to get in touch with this Primo. I saw him going into a building where raw materials like cement and blocks were kept. I made an excuse to the foreman that I had to get something there and I followed him in. When I caught up with him, I asked him in my broken German and Yiddish if I could talk to him for a minute. I told him that the Auschwitz Underground needed his help. He told me that he didn't want to be involved with the Underground, that I was wasting my time.

That was the end of our conversation. But the Underground didn't give up so easily. "Press him again," they said. They sent me there a second time and I found him again, but he still insisted that he didn't want to be involved. "I'm not ready for the gas chamber or for the Mosquito *Kommando*," he said. I didn't know what he was talking about at the time and was disappointed that he was rejecting me again. I told him that I was only a messenger and that he was risking his life by saying no to those guys. Primo asked what exactly they wanted from him. I explained that when he was inside the factory, he might receive a little package from a British soldier. He would then pass the package to someone like me. I somehow managed to persuade him to relay a package once or twice. It was only once or twice because he refused to do it any more than that. It seems that the Underground didn't continue to pressure him after that.

When the Underground saw that I wasn't afraid to do these types of things, they decided that I would receive some packages directly from the Count of Auschwitz myself. They told me that he would be wearing a military uniform and that he would recognize me by the fact that I would be wearing my hat differently. He would pass a package to me that I would hide inside my shirt. They told me not to ask questions. I really didn't want to do it, but I remembered what kapo Manfred had told me about the power of the Underground.

I didn't go to Buna every day, maybe just once or twice a week. They probably didn't have these missions for us to do every day. But when Ziggy took his next hundred guys out to work in Buna, there were five or six of us there who belonged to the Underground. Ziggy put me to work in a ditch, digging and repairing pipes and fitting them together. There were hundreds of people around. The place was enormous. And there were two or three SS with guns guarding us.

On one occasion, I saw some British soldiers approaching us. When they reached the ditch where I was working, one of the men jumped in and started yelling at me that I wasn't doing the job right. All of a sudden, I felt him slip something inside my uniform. It was the Baron. The second time he gave me a package, the Baron pointed his finger at me. "For you. For you." He spoke German. I knew the package was supposed to be for me. What did he mean? Then I realized that there was something special for me in the package. I was getting to be a little less dim by that time and it took maybe two seconds for me to make the connection. When I opened up the package I saw two cigarettes wrapped in paper. In the camps this meant I was a millionaire. I knew what to do with the cigarettes right away.

When I got back to the barracks I told Jakob what I had. He suggested that I give him one in case the guards caught me and I lost it. That was a good idea. We split them up and traded the cigarettes for some food. By this time, they had taken Jakob to another barracks. I only saw him once in a while in the evening and we would exchange stories about work.

One day, Jakob brought me something to wear. He had gotten it from the Kanada *Kommando*, where he worked. He soon started bringing all types of things from Kanada to sell and trade in the barracks. We started a new business together and it felt like we were tycoons. Now that I was working for the Underground and I was getting extra goods from the Baron, I felt like I had new blood running through me. Suddenly I felt like a human being again and no longer so degraded. It was like an injection of life.

Despite the new energy and hope that I got from working for the Underground, I also experienced an example of how powerful and how vicious they could be. One day, when I got a package from the Baron, I found another few cigarettes. Getting the cigarettes was one of the best things that could happen, but holding on to them was one of the worst. There wasn't anywhere safe to put them. I slept with five people. That night, I hardly slept, trying not to squash the cigarettes. I decided that to make my life easier, instead of trading one cigarette each day for soup, which is what I had been doing, it might be a good idea to give one of the cooks a couple of cigarettes and tell him that I want five or six soups. That way, every day, Jakob and I could get a little extra soup and I wouldn't have to worry about hanging on to the cigarettes.

The next day, when I got my soup, I gave the guy two cigarettes and I said, "You know me. Here's the two cigarettes and I want five or six extra soups." He took the cigarettes and said okay. The day after that I got my regular soup and I ate it up then waited for another soup. I had to wait until the soup line ended and everyone was served. Then the cook's buddies could get their extra soup. Any bit extra when we were that hungry was a bonus. It was not so much for our stomachs as for our minds. So when it came to the end of the line and everybody had already gone, I said, "Now give me mine." I was sure there was another cup of soup left.

Instead of giving me my promised soup, the cook took the ladle and hit me right in the face. Blood was flowing so profusely down my face that I had to cup my face with my hand. We had nothing to heal a wound with except cold water. I ran to the washroom and put my head under the tap until the bleeding stopped. It wasn't such a deep cut, but when the blood dried I was left with a scar. I went back to the barracks and when I saw Jakob later, he was flabbergasted. After getting a cigarette and holding it a whole night without any sleep, losing it like this and then getting hit in the face was unforgivable.

The next evening, when the Poles from the Underground saw me, they didn't like the looks of it. They nodded to me and one of them asked me what the mark on my face was and who had done it to me. I explained that I had received a couple of cigarettes with the package from the Baron and that I gave them to the guy serving the food and this was what he did. "He was supposed to pay me with an extra soup, but he clobbered me instead," I said.

They told me not to go to Buna the next day. They were concerned that my injuries would make me too noticeable. I knew how dangerous this business was. If I got caught, I would get a bullet right on the spot or they would send me to the gas chamber. I mean, a bullet would be a blessing but I knew that first they would interrogate me and other people might get beaten too. I knew that I was risking my life. But I also knew that if I was going to get anything extra, there was nothing that could stop me. So when they told me not to go, I was really disappointed.

Two nights later, I came in from work and I saw a new guy dishing out the soup. The one who had hit me was gone. I asked the other men what had happened to the other guy. "He was found with his throat cut," they said. The Underground didn't play games.

When I didn't work at Buna, kapo Manfred was good to me and my job was always open with him. He could take as many people as he wanted. No kapo was told how many men he needed. The Germans had so many people they didn't care. There were, at any given time, about a quarter of a million labourers in Auschwitz.

Whenever the Underground needed someone to take a package from Buna to Birkenau, I was told to join Ziggy's *Kommando*. We walked through the main gate of the D camp past the guards and the SS counted us. When we came back in the evening, we were counted again and we were searched thoroughly since we were coming from Buna. Even kapo Ziggy was searched because there was war materiel at Buna and they worried that there might be sabotage. So the question was what to do with the package before we passed the guards.

Approximately halfway down the road between Buna and Birkenau was the Kanada *Kommando*. When the women who worked in Kanada came back into their camp, the guards didn't always bother to search them very thoroughly. Sometimes, when the guards wanted something for themselves, they even asked the women to bring it.

Around Birkenau there was construction work going on all the time and during the construction provisional toilets were set up for people to use. One of these washrooms was outside of Kanada, for people like us who were walking along the road. It was for both men and women, divided by a piece of plywood. We could practically see the women on the other side. This toilet was the drop-off point.

The Underground explained the procedure: "On the way home, you're going to use this toilet and leave the package from the Baron beside the toilet. A woman will come in after you and take this package away." That was my assignment. Kapo Ziggy knew all about the plan and he put me in such a position that I wasn't visible. In any case, nobody was really paying attention. People had one thought on their minds: how to get through the day without being hit or killed. When I had the package, I went to the washroom. The women from Kanada who worked for the Underground were watching. They knew that one of the men going to the washroom would have something. One of these women would come and knock on the washroom door. She would say, "Have you got it?" in Yiddish. And if the man wasn't a runner, he wouldn't know what to answer, so she would go away. The Poles told me that if I saw that there was any danger, I should throw the package into the toilet. They warned me not to try to be a hero. When I was in the toilet and a woman knocked at the door, I could see her through the cracks. If a man knocked after I went in, I had to throw the package down the hole because I knew he didn't belong. I couldn't leave it and I wouldn't have a chance to go back. This was very important because it was so dangerous. I made maybe fifteen or twenty trips to Buna and of those trips, I succeeded in receiving packages maybe five or six times and only once did I have to dump the package in the toilet because nobody came for it.

When I had a package, I would leave it in a corner and go out. The woman would come in, take the package and go back to Kanada to finish up her work. At night, she brought the package in through the gate and somehow passed it on to the Underground. From what I heard later, the women also got tiny packages of gunpowder from other runners who worked in the Union factory, a munitions plant near the main Auschwitz camp. The women who brought the packages from the Union factory into the camp gave them to other women in the Kanada *Kommando* who were also picked by the Underground. The women in the Kanada *Kommando* wrapped the gunpowder in pieces of paper or cotton and stashed it in their uniforms. That was the way they took it into their barracks.

The end of one of the women's barracks was close to Crematorium I, but separated by an electric wire. At night, over time, men from the *Sonderkommando* working in the crematorium dug a hole under the wire. The women left the packages on their side, next to the fence and a guy risked his life by crawling on his belly to grab them. That's how gunpowder ended up in the crematoria and made it possible for the *Sonderkommando* to revolt. The Germans didn't catch them, and the whole operation nearly succeeded.

Uprising

The Underground had been working with the *Sonderkommando* for a while to organize resistance. As I mentioned earlier, the *Sonderkommando* had to deal with the dead bodies of prisoners; when they were sent to work in the crematoria they too were already condemned to die – because of their work, what they witnessed, the Germans only kept them alive for a period of time. Because there was no shortage of Jews, they didn't have to keep the same ones. But they always needed a few experienced people to teach the new ones what to do, so they left a few men there who became kapos. Maybe later on they got rid of them. I don't know. In each crematorium I think there was one kapo in charge, with numerous *Sonderkommando* prisoners under him and maybe a few foremen.

There were four crematoria in Birkenau. Crematoria I and II had grounds close together, III and IV were on the same grounds and then there were the ditches. By the end of the summer of 1944, the *Sonderkommando* at Crematorium III knew that they were soon going to be killed, and the Jewish kapo there, in collaboration with the Underground, formed a plot to blow up the facility. I don't know how or if the prisoners working in Crematorium III got in touch with the prisoners at the other crematoria to let them know that something was going to happen but from what I understand, plans were somehow being made for an uprising.

There had been a terrible selection of Jews in the camp at the end of September 1944. A lot of people went to the gas chambers and I really don't know how I was spared. We had to go in through one washroom, walk past Mengele, and the ones who weren't chosen had to go in to another washroom. I was free to go back to my regular work with kapo Manfred and I remember working near the Gypsy barracks. By this time, the Gypsies had been murdered. Sometime in August, a transport from Lodz had arrived and those who didn't go to the gas chamber went to the Gypsy camp. I was always trying to get near there because I thought that maybe I could find somebody I knew from Lodz. I happened to also be there when the uprising started.

At the time, I didn't know about the planning of the uprising. I'll tell you what happened from what I know. I don't know if it's all true, mind you. I want you to know that this is what I heard from one of the *Sonderkommando* who took part in it and whom I met later. There are probably other versions of this story, but I have to tell what I know and what I heard from the horse's mouth.

Sometime in March or April 1944 they began to be very busy at the crematoria and the ovens never stopped; they were working round the clock. The Hungarian Jews, the Jews from Lodz, the Jews from France and from Belgium were coming in massive transports, one after the other. In the summer following this increased activity, I started to have a strong feeling that something was up. After all, I was smuggling packages from Buna, so I guessed something was going to happen, but I didn't know what – I didn't know that there would be an uprising on October 7, 1944. As a matter of fact, it wasn't supposed to be October 7. That's part of the reason that the uprising didn't go off as planned.

All around Auschwitz was countryside with lots of trees and fields. The Polish Home Army had somehow arranged with the Auschwitz Underground that on a certain date they would be close to the camp and would need a signal so they could make a surprise attack on the SS guards. It was decided that the Underground should blow up one of the crematoria as the signal. When the crematorium blew up, the Home Army would cut the electric wires and enter the camp. The Underground, along with prisoners in the camp, would seize and kill the German guards.

By August 1944, there were about 135,000 inmates at Auschwitz, Birkenau and Buna-Monowitz. The majority were women, but there were those who, even in their weakened state, were ready to fight anybody and anything, especially Germans. An Auschwitz inmate was no longer just any ordinary inmate. Many of us were ready to go and kill Germans with our bare hands, even knowing we would be killed ourselves. Our hate was so powerful that we didn't even care if we were going to die. As a matter of fact, I remember that toward the end of the war, areas near Auschwitz were bombed once or twice and we were happy. Why didn't they bomb the crematoria and us together? We were begging for this.

The Underground knew that if they could get enough people like this going, they could form a small fighting force. There were also some soldiers in Auschwitz who could be helpful, too. On top of that, there were the factories, like Buna-Werke and I. G. Farben, and there were the hospitals – they thought they would be able to get everything they needed for a battle. But they needed a surprise attack to succeed.

The Germans, from what I heard later on, had dissolved most of the ghettos and were running out of Jews to bring into the camps. After all the activity of the spring, they didn't need the crematoria as much as they did before. Aside from this, although we didn't know it at the time, the Soviet army had already advanced into Poland. The German authorities at Auschwitz had received an order from Berlin to start shutting the camp down, starting with killing the inmates who knew the most, the *Sonderkommando*. When this became clear to the *Sonderkommando*, they knew they had to act quickly, or they would be killed before they had a chance to carry out their mission. Even though the timing was still being figured out, they knew what they were supposed to do with the supply of gunpowder. But they jumped the gun.

They knew that their time was short because the Germans had shot the Jewish kapo from Crematorium I and, soon after that, there was a big selection of *Sonderkommando* workers. The prisoners who saw this started to get panicky. On the day of the uprising, there was no communication with the rest of the *Sonderkommando* in the other crematoria. When the Germans next came for the *Sonderkommando*, some of them decided to put up a fight right away. The Germans began shooting and these men fought back. They grabbed whatever was at hand – sticks, bricks – and began shouting and fighting. The Germans called for more guards and the guards came with dogs and more guns.

I think it was maybe ten or eleven o'clock in the morning when I heard an explosion. We all looked up. A crematorium was exploding and burning. The *Sonderkommando* at Crematoria III must have set off their gunpowder, which started a fire. Crematorium III started burning. All this happened in a matter of half an hour to an hour.

From my vantage point near the Gypsy camp, it seemed to me that two of the crematoria were burning – I can still see it in my mind's eye – but I know now that only Crematorium III burned to the ground. I also know that because of this, transports temporarily stopped coming to Auschwitz.

The outbreak in the crematorium was premature because it turned out that the Polish Home Army wasn't yet ready to act. Some of the *Sonderkommando* from Crematoria III, however, still managed to cut the electric wire and escape. The rest were shot on the spot. In the end, the ones who escaped were also caught. From what I heard later, the Germans found them in a cabin about ten kilometres from Birkenau, surrounded it and attacked them with flame-throwers. Most of the *Sonderkommando* from Crematoria III were killed that day. But I was told by some of the *Sonderkommando* from Crematoria I who survived, and who I later got to know, that they caught one of the German kapos and threw him alive into the ovens. Either because of lack of communication or because the SS moved quickly to shut things down, the *Sonderkommando* in Crematoria II and IV didn't take part in the uprising at all.

Nothing happened to me at first. I finished my work and went back to the barracks. By then, everything was quiet. The only thing I saw were Germans, driving trucks that were bringing back the *Sonderkommando* who had escaped; they were dead. It was a shock for all of us. We hadn't known about the plans. It was apparently also a shock for the SS that in their pet camp, the pride and joy of the Third Reich, one of the crematoria could be blown up. Even more so, however, I can only imagine that it was a shock for the Nazi leadership in Berlin, especially Reichsführer Himmler.

It didn't take them long to figure out about the gunpowder. They realized that somebody must have smuggled it in. Who was going from the various camps and factories to Birkenau? The very first man the Gestapo arrested when they came into the D camp after the uprising was kapo Ziggy. There were others, but they knew of him and they took him first because he was a Jewish kapo. They asked him how many times he had brought the explosives into the camp. He said he didn't know anything. They told him to give them the names of all the men who worked with him.

The SS went around to the barracks with Ziggy, an officer keeping his rifle pointed at Ziggy's back. That showed us that kapo Ziggy was in trouble, but hardly anybody knew why. They were going from barracks to barracks because he said he didn't remember anyone's names, he only remembered faces. Little by little he pointed out a few hundred men to the SS, including me. I still wasn't sure what it was all about, but I had a hunch.

They took us to the main building of the Birkenau office. A high-ranking officer came out and talked to kapo Ziggy for a few minutes. Then he took out a revolver and shot him right in front of us. We were stunned. They had shot kapo Ziggy and maybe they were going to shoot us too. But still, nobody knew why for sure, though I guessed by then that it was something to do with the burning crematorium.

They announced that they were going to interrogate us.

After the SS shot Ziggy, they assembled all the men who had gone from Birkenau to Buna on work details – in all, they had rounded up a few hundred prisoners. Other kapos were also taken since Ziggy couldn't name all the names and the SS didn't want to miss anyone. They divided us into groups of five and took us to an SS barracks, a *Schreibstube*, for interrogation. Before even beginning the interrogation, two SS came in and started torturing us. They started beating me over the head, left and right. Soon my left eye was hanging out so that I had to take my hand and push it back in again. I can't see out of that eye anymore. Luckily it wasn't severed altogether, so my eye was saved, but there's no sight in it. I was bleeding from my eye, my nose and my body and then I passed out.

I was lucky. They left me at the *Schreibstube* while they sent the rest to Block 11 for interrogation. I was unconscious for maybe a day. It was night when I finally got up, but I really don't remember if it was the same night or the next night. I came to in a pool of blood and it wasn't just my blood. There were many other guys lying around. I don't know how many were living or dead. When the SS went around and kicked the bodies, they saw that I was still alive. They dragged me out with a group of about fifty people and they tortured us some more. Some of the men in the group died right away. Soon there was shooting all around me, and people were killed left and right.

Meanwhile, from where I was, I could hear the telephones ringing and the voices of the women operators yelling to the officers to take calls from the administration in Berlin. The officers didn't want to talk to the officials in Berlin, who wanted to know if they had caught the guilty parties and killed them. In fact, the officials didn't know who was who. They didn't know where to start.

An SS officer hauled me to a bench where there was a vice. He took one of my fingers, put it in the vice and asked me in German if I had been at Buna. "Buna?" I answered. I wasn't going to admit I was there. If he was asking me, that meant he wasn't sure. I just shrugged and got hit over the head. He kept asking me and hitting me. This went on and on, but I wouldn't say anything. I had been a veteran for too long. If I'd said, "Yes," I'd be dead already. If I didn't admit anything, then I might have a chance. By the fifth or sixth time I said nothing, he started tearing out my fingernails. I screamed and passed out. I'm lucky that I faint easily. I was plain unconscious.

The SS man revived me with a pail of water and when I came to he asked again, "Are you going to tell us? Where did you get explosives? Who was in charge? Who did you give it to?"

He grabbed another fingernail. I probably would have started talking but I fainted again. After a few fingernails he gave up. One nail is completely gone now. A few are partially gone. It's not easy to tear out fingernails and this guy was not an expert, just a plain, ordinary SS man. Some of the nails he tore out more, some he tore out less. But I was already in such pain that I resigned myself that either he was going to shoot me or he was going to take more fingernails so I just fainted.

After that ordeal was over I was left on the ground with a bunch of other guys. There was blood everywhere and nobody bothered us for awhile. Two of the men near me had been shot and many others soon died from the torture. We were there for quite awhile, maybe a few days, with no food or water and nobody came in to talk to us for that time.

Imagine lying on a concrete floor, bleeding, in perpetual darkness. I didn't know if it was day or night. We were in a little room with small windows high up. There were several chairs, a bench and a table. There was an electric lamp hanging from the ceiling, which was only on when the SS came in, which they soon did again. At first, they interrogated prisoners one at a time, but later they took more of us together. I don't know if they planned it this way but it was definitely worse.

More than once, they tortured five or six inmates to death right in front of me. The only thing that was worse was hearing the screaming and crying from the hallways or the next room. It was clear that nobody could help us. I knew I was going to die and I only hoped it would be sooner rather than later. Even though I was not a big believer, I tried repeating prayers from memory to whatever God there was.

Finally it came to a point where they didn't get anything from us. My sense of time was vague but after what was probably a few days, they came in to take all of us out. They wanted to see who was able to walk. There were about fifteen or twenty of us who were able to get up after the torture.

From what I know, of the few hundred rounded up for interrogation and tortured, there were only two or three men who were runners for the Underground like I was. The rest of them were innocent people who just happened to go to work at Buna. The two Polish inmates who were my link to the Underground were also there. I only remember the name of one of them, Vlad. He was very good to me, trying his best to stop the bleeding and helping me later. When we got a little bit better physically, he worked closely with me because he knew me and wanted me to survive. He also gave me a lot of information. The other Pole died during the interrogation.

If this chapter of my story is confusing, believe me, it was hard for me to figure out and write about. Think about where I was and what had happened to me in those few days. Every event of those days is like a nightmare, even today, especially at night. I still feel the pain, mentally and physically. Whenever I think about this part of my life, I start getting anxious. I hallucinate so that I imagine that I'm talking about somebody else and my wife has to bring me back to reality.

∽

I was surprised that I was still alive. They put us together in groups of five and put us in a truck. I was sure they were going to take us to be shot. Instead, they took us to work in Crematoria III and IV to clean up. Crematoria III had been practically burned to the ground. Some pieces were just sticking out. I was half-dead and couldn't even climb onto the truck. If Vlad hadn't given me a push, the guard probably would have shot me. During the next few weeks of working on the clean-up, Vlad explained much of what was supposed to have happened and what did happen, up until the uprising. I asked him why I hadn't known that there were other Jews in the Underground. He said that it was because the Jewish prisoners were all destined for the gas chamber. "If you knew what was going to happen to you in a few hours," he explained, "wouldn't you try to save your life by telling what you knew about the Underground?"

I also asked Vlad about kapo Ziggy and he told me what he knew. He probably didn't know everything himself. What he told me was that Ziggy had been a volunteer in the Spanish Civil War. He also belonged to the German Communist Party. After Kristallnacht, when the Germans started arresting Jews, they arrested him. They released him, but he was under the surveillance of the Gestapo. Still, Ziggy and a friend managed to get on the *St. Louis*, which, as I've said, didn't succeed in finding a place to dock with all the Jewish refugees on board. He landed in a country that was later occupied by Germany, I don't know which one, and was arrested. But nobody knows if he was arrested because he was involved in sabotage or he was arrested just because he was a Jew. Ziggy was then sent to one of the concentration camps. It could have been Dachau or Mauthausen. Auschwitz hadn't been built at the beginning of the war. When Auschwitz was built, the Germans transferred inmates there from other camps and that's how Ziggy ended up in Auschwitz, where he became a kapo.

According to Vlad, kapo Ziggy organized some of the smuggling that I was involved in. Vlad thought that he was also the one who had developed the relationship with the Count of Auschwitz. Why kapo Ziggy was killed by the Gestapo officer without being interrogated, according to Vlad, was a mystery. Why didn't they wait until they took us inside? Why didn't they torture him if he knew so much? There are so many unanswered questions.

I came to my own conclusions as to why Ziggy was shot. I think that the officer who shot Ziggy was in cahoots with him about the work assignments. Kapo Ziggy, after all, was more than an ordinary kapo. If he survived that long in the camps as a German Jew, he must have been very clever. He must have known who to talk to, like the way he knew kapo Manfred. He probably bribed SS officers who knew the war was going to end soon. Whether they won or lost the war, it was better to be rich than poor; it's even possible deals were made with gold and diamonds looted from the arriving transports. The officer who shot Ziggy perhaps did so because he knew Ziggy would be tortured and might give up some information about him. Or maybe he liked Ziggy and wanted to be merciful. This is only my own opinion.

I hardly even remember sitting on the truck that took us to clean up the crematoria. I was bleeding from my head, from my hands and from my eyes. I was so beaten up that I was wetting myself. Nevertheless, I had seen an officer kick one of our guys to get up for work and when the guy didn't move they shot him. I was going to be next. It took all the energy I had, but, with Vlad's help, I had gotten up and into that truck. I regret that I lost contact with Vlad. I never even knew what happened to him or where he ended up.

Crematorium III was pretty much demolished. It was full of puddles of water from when the fire had been doused. When we got there we saw that there were still fire trucks being used – fire trucks being pulled by people, not by cars, not even by horses. When the smoke was finally completely out, they left. The Germans didn't want anybody to know too much about what was going on. They didn't want just any inmates cleaning up the crematoria. Since they were probably going to shoot those of us who had already been interrogated and tortured anyway, they figured they could use us to clean up the crematoria first. There was a lot to do. There were bodies all around. For the first time, I saw how huge the crematoria complexes were. I saw the gas chambers, bunkers, ovens, experiment rooms and all the *Magazines*, warehouses.

I still hadn't eaten, but I wasn't very hungry. There was water from the puddles left after the fire and that's all we had. I could hardly do anything. An SS officer gave us orders to start cleaning up. They brought in a few other men because they saw we were dying. A man I recognized as a runner for the Underground died later on, so I may have been the only one left who was actually from the guilty party. We worked there for two or three days and slept in the ruins of the crematoria.

The only thing that I could do was kick things with my feet. I could hardly see. I was holding my eye. I was still bleeding from my fingernails. Blood was running from my hand. I couldn't touch anything because my fingers were swollen and the tips were raw. All of us were in this kind of shape, but the work got done. We cleaned up all the debris and it was transported away in trucks.

Now I was waiting to be shot, like everybody else had been. In a situation like this, none of us expected to live another minute, but we did. In the evening a truck came around and they put us in it and said, "Okay, it's finished now." We figured that was all they needed from us and now they were going to take us to the gas chamber or they were going to shoot us. Instead, they took us to the grounds of the other crematoria.

They put us in a room where all the workers from the crematoria used to live; they apparently planned to use us to clean up the other crematoria. Some of the *Sonderkommando* who had been involved in the uprising were marched out as we looked on. These men knew they were going to be killed so as they marched out, they sang a song. I didn't know, in all that time in Auschwitz, that people could march and sing. We weren't allowed to sing. The Germans lined them up in rows of five and the men started singing very loudly, over and over, the same four verses. That's the first time I remember hearing "The Song of the Partisans." I remember those men, the way they left that day, so proudly singing that song.

A few of the *Sonderkommando* workers, as well as some of the kapos, remained. I remember the names of two of these kapos: Phillipe, I think, was a French Jew and a man we called Lemke was a Lithuanian. Lemke told us what to do. "Guys," he said, "we've won another few days of relief." He told us that Phillipe would give us our work assignments and then he would take us back to the camp. Maybe we would have a chance to survive. Lemke had been in the crematorium before the rebellion and he told me more about the uprising.

When we heard the "Song of the Partisans," I asked Lemke about it. He told us this story. There was a Lithuanian rabbi who knew the young man who wrote the song. They were together in the Vilnius ghetto. The rabbi was sent to Auschwitz and the composer, who had joined the partisans, was killed. The rabbi brought the song to Auschwitz and ended up in the crematorium with the *Sonderkommando*, so he taught it to them. I think that was the first time the song was officially sung at Auschwitz. The men from the *Sonderkommando* had to march through the whole length of D camp and they sang this song continuously, for everybody to hear. That was the last of them.

It was the end of November 1944 when we were told to stop cleaning up – apparently an order came from Berlin to start demolishing the remaining crematoria instead. We were also to clean up and demolish the first killing unit at Auschwitz – the ditches and the bunker at the little farmhouse – and put grass around there. The Germans knew the Soviets were close by so they wanted to clean up the evidence. So, after we had dismantled Crematoria III and cleaned up around the ditches, they took us to Crematorium II to get rid of the ashes. Each crematorium had a pile of human ashes. The crematoria burned everything from the bodies, but there were always big bones left over. Those remains hadn't been taken away before the uprising happened. According to Lemke, they had to be crushed, put into burlap sacks and hauled away to be dumped.

I was one of the guys who took these ashes in a truck with an SS driver and another SS guard. We drove to the places where we were dumping the ashes but we kept the burlap to use again; the Germans didn't throw anything away. At first, because they didn't want too many witnesses, we threw the ashes into the Vistula River, about five or six kilometres away from the camp, far enough away from the town that nobody would see. Later, when they didn't have enough time to go so far and didn't care anymore, we drove only a kilometre or so right into Oświęcim and stopped the truck on a bridge in the middle of the city. We went down under the bridge to dispose of the ashes in the little Soła River, with the SS guarding us with machine guns. We were hardly able to walk, never mind run away, but they were watching us. I think I must have done this three or four times. Mind you, there was still a lot left, but by my last trip it wasn't such a big pile.

On January 5, 1945, nobody went to work. They hanged four girls who had collaborated with the Underground by helping to provide the *Sonderkommando* with gunpowder. One was the courier and three of them worked in the powder factory. The whole women's camp had to watch along with other inmates suspected of taking part in the uprising. They hanged them in two shifts – two of the girls during the day and the other two at night.

The entire time this was happening, Jakob was still working in Kanada. He told me that in Kanada the Germans were trying to clear up everything they could, moving out all the gold and other treasures. There weren't any more transports, so nothing much was arriving. The Germans were just removing whatever they could.

Leaving Auschwitz

By January 1945, there were approximately 64,000 thousand inmates left in all of the Auschwitz camps. The Soviets were close by – at night we saw lights flashing in the sky and we thought we could hear cannons.

One day, the SS told us to get up early in the morning and assemble in front of the barracks, just as if we were going out to work. There were no lights from the towers. Some guys snuck by the electric wire and found that it was cut. There was no electricity. Now we were afraid. There were rumours we were going to be shot or hanged and that there weren't going to be any survivors. We still didn't know what was going on. Were they going to shoot us?

The SS then announced that whoever couldn't walk would have to remain in the camp. We didn't know it, but we were about to start out on the infamous Death March. A few thousand sick people remained in the camp, despite the fact that the SS said that they were going to kill anybody who stayed behind. As we were leaving, we waved to those who remained; they were crying and waving to us. I went on the march.

On January 18, 1945, I left Auschwitz. That was a very memorable day for me because I hadn't expected to come out of there alive. I remember when we, I mean almost the whole of Auschwitz-Birkenau, marched out of the camp. The march started with a very slow tempo and when Jakob and I passed the main gate of Birkenau I looked up to the sky in the direction of Crematoria I and II and I could still see the chimneys. It took a few moments to realize that they were not really there anymore. We were leaving Auschwitz, but not through the chimneys after all. I pointed it out to Jakob. He stopped and turned towards me and shook my shoulders. "Wake up. We've seen enough as it is," he said.

A few large groups went out that day. I later learned that some of them ended up in Dachau. I didn't know it then, but I was with a group of men who were headed for Mauthausen, in Austria. There were some 6,000 of us. We had only our prison uniforms on. Jakob had an extra jacket and sweater. I had the shoes from Kanada that he had given me before. As we left the D camp, we passed the warehouse. Some people ahead of us made a rush for the *Magazines* and for the kitchens. The SS were guarding us, but people were running in and out of line trying to get whatever they could.

Two Germans were standing with their guns in front of the warehouse. I told Jakob to walk slowly and I would catch up with him. Before he could try to stop me, I ran out of the line and into the warehouse to have a look around. I saw a sealed can and I grabbed it. I didn't even know what was in it. It was a heavy industrial can that restaurants and the military use. I knew I had to be quick because I heard shooting. I stashed the can under my uniform and ran out. There was plenty of confusion and the two German guards were too busy shooting and yelling to notice me.

I looked around for Jakob and saw him waving. He was moving with the rest but trying to slow down.

"Where did you go? What have you got there?" he asked when I caught up with him.

"I got a can," I told him. "I don't know what it is. I can't hold it. It's cold." It was the middle of winter and I was freezing so we shared the burden of carrying it. It had taken me about 20 seconds to run in and out and all I could grab was that sealed can, but I didn't want to let it go.

We walked the whole day on the highway. If trucks and cars

passed, we had to go into the ditches. Most of them were military trucks. I don't think we saw any private vehicles. We kept walking through the entire night and all of the next day. We finally rested the next evening in a huge field of snow. There were so many of us that when we lay down I could no longer see the snow. We still had no food and nothing to drink, just snow.

The next morning, before we continued on, we heard a voice through a megaphone telling us, "Anyone who can't keep up will be shot. You're better off to stay here where you'll be safe." But we all knew that if we stayed we would be shot anyway, so naturally everybody tried to go on – even those who had come sick and half-naked from the camp hospitals, where they had likely been experimented on. But those ones didn't last long, hardly dressed, with no food, marching in winter, lying all night in snow and then marching again. They slowed down. When they couldn't march anymore, they were shot.

We plowed on for seven or eight days. We were eating snow and sleeping on snow. Poland has very harsh winters. We walked and the SS rode or walked behind us. Every few feet lay another body, another corpse. Either they dropped and were shot, or they tried to run away. Quite a few people ran away. I just didn't have the energy to run. There was no place to go. We could hear artillery, which meant the front was near.

Finally we came to a big field and the Germans told us to lie down. We needed rest more than food or anything else because we were so exhausted. Not too far from us there was an old burned-out barn. Jakob suggested we go there because it provided a little bit of shelter. I couldn't get up because I was so weak, so Jakob helped me and, together with another prisoner, we crawled into a corner of the barn.

Now we were really hungry. We hadn't eaten for days. I still had the can with me and I still didn't know what was in it, but I figured it must be food. I said to Jakob, "How are we going to open this can?" Our fingers were frozen. We were lying under a broken-down roof with planks hanging down from the walls and the ceiling.

Jakob said, "I have an idea, Felix. I see a big nail." He pointed to a board with a big rusty nail stuck in it. Jakob then got up and broke off a piece of the plank and took the nail out. He put the point of the nail against the can and banged it with a piece of wood. We worked on it in turns with our other friend. It wasn't easy. This was a heavy metal can. It took us the whole night to punch those little holes. Finally we made an opening big enough to put a finger in to see what was inside.

We didn't think it was juice because it was too heavy, so probably it was potatoes or meat. We were hoping for meat. It was my can, so I went first. My fingers were frozen. The can was frozen. When I put my fingers in, I felt scratching. My fingers were bleeding but I didn't feel pain because of the cold. There was a little bit of liquid that was frozen and it melted on my fingers. I didn't know for sure if my fingers were wet from the contents of the can or from my own blood. I pulled out a piece of meat! When I put that piece of meat in my mouth, I felt alive again. In my mind I already felt stronger and had a will to live.

Piece by piece we dug the meat out and we ate this for two days. Opening this can probably saved our lives. The Germans didn't give us any food while we were on the march. With new energy, we managed to walk to Bratislava, Czechoslovakia. We saw it was Bratislava because we saw the name of the city at the train station as we went by. By then we had finished the meat. The local people came close by and saw the shape we were in. They didn't have much themselves, but they threw some bread and potatoes at us. Some Germans started shooting at them. The people were yelling and still throwing bread at us, to whoever could grab it. I wasn't close enough to get any.

For about a day, thousands of us sat in Bratislava in a field right by the railroad tracks. Then the Germans put us in open cattle cars. There were some Red Cross people observing nearby, so the German soldiers gave us pieces of bread while we were boarding the trains. We saw quite a few people left who couldn't manage to move and probably some of them were dead.

The train started moving, leaving Bratislava. I ate my bread and my neighbour ate his. I saw another guy hadn't eaten his bread so I nudged him and said, "Why aren't you eating?" He was already dead. So I took his bread and shared it with Jakob.

A day later, the train arrived in Mauthausen, in Austria. I had never heard of Mauthausen but there were some guys from other places who had and one said, "Oh, Mauthausen, that's another killer camp." I was too hungry and too frozen to even think about it. When we got off the cattle cars it was terribly cold. We were still wearing our ordinary striped uniforms. On the way there I had found another jacket that was too big for me. Jakob still had his light jacket and sweater. That was all we had.

As we left the train I saw that a number of people were lying motionless in the cattle car. We had been squeezed so tightly together that nobody knew who was dead or alive. When we had gotten food, I had seen some bread on the ground. People hadn't eaten for ten days and now they couldn't eat and just dropped the food. Both Jakob and I picked it up. I don't know how many died, but I know that I left the train with quite a few pieces of bread. I would estimate that in the end at least 30 per cent of the people who managed to leave the cattle cars also didn't make it. If they weren't dead, they were dying.

They took us to Mauthausen concentration camp, which was outside the city. When we walked through the city the people pretended that we didn't exist. I guess for them it was not a novelty. They were shaking their heads, as if they knew, "These guys are not going to live long." I could see it in their faces. Not even one of them offered us a little bit of water and by now there were not too many Germans keeping an eye on us – maybe a couple of hundred for a few thousand of us. Still, whoever couldn't walk was shot.

Later I found out what happened to those who had died on the road to Mauthausen. There is a special cemetery not far from the camp where the citizens of Mauthausen dug a mass grave. Nobody knew who the dead were or what nationality they were. But there's a grave there with a big cross.

It was not so easy to walk from the station to the camp. I don't remember how far it was, but it was uphill because the camp was on the mountain. Every step was pure torture. Finally we made it up to the camp. I didn't think I'd be able to make it another hundred feet. Jakob was holding me up and I was holding Jakob and another guy was holding him. We stumbled up to the gate of Mauthausen with the SS right behind us. Every few metres we saw another dead body on the ground, shot.

At the gate of Mauthausen they took us in, five by five. The Mauthausen SS made a selection. Another selection! I couldn't fathom it. Why would they make a selection now, of dead people? Why not go ahead and shoot us all? We all looked the same. But they did. I think it was by force of habit. They were still selecting who would go to the gas chambers. To be honest with you, by then I didn't even care where I was going. We all looked so haggard and so old and so miserable. They had to look close into our eyes to see how old we were. If someone was more than thirty, they couldn't survive in this camp. About twenty-five people were sent to the gas chamber right away, after all they'd been through. I don't know how I made it. I was half dead. I still hadn't recuperated from the torture. I was starving, weak and frozen. My only strength was in my mind. Everyone was a skeleton. There was no part of my body where I could feel flesh. Those other guys must have looked really dead.

We had no idea what was going to happen next. They had us undress and they put us in showers. When I saw the shower, I thought it was going to be gas, but it was a real shower with hot water. We were so thirsty that we were drinking hot water from the showers. We wanted to stay in there; they had to chase us out. Then we were given hot soup, the first hot soup in about two weeks. Then we were given new clothes and put in the barracks for a rest. Three days later, they put us to work in the Mauthausen quarry.

The guys who were already there and knew what to do were splitting rocks. The rest of us were supposed to carry these rocks out of the quarry. I didn't know where to go. I saw prisoners going up steps and I said to myself, "Up these steps carrying rocks on my shoulder? I can't make it." There were about a hundred and eighty steps. If a thousand people went down for rocks, maybe five hundred survived the hundred and eighty steps back up. If they lost their balance, the fall would kill them. If they didn't go straight up, the kapos and the SS hit them. The guards gave them one over the head and if they fell down from the top stair, it was over for them. This was our initiation to Mauthausen. I looked at this and I looked at Jakob as if to say, "Did we survive for this?" They didn't need these rocks. I don't know what they were doing with them. I think it was only for pure torture. Somehow we both survived that day in the quarry.

The next day, Jakob landed a job splitting rocks, which at least was a little bit easier. He could stay down at the bottom of the quarry. I thought I would never see him again because I didn't think I'd be able to make it up the stairs with the rocks. But I made it. I don't know how. Jakob came into the barracks after we returned from work and he was happy to see me still alive.

I lasted three days at the quarry. On the third day, Jakob got up in the morning very slowly. He could hardly walk. He then nudged me to get up. I said, "I'm not going."

He said, "You have to go. Otherwise they're going to shoot you right away or send you to the gas chamber."

"I can't go any more," I declared. "I don't want to die in the quarry. If they want to shoot me here, it's better than that." I looked at him and I saw three Jakobs. I felt dizzy and I knew I wouldn't be able to walk. I didn't want to tell him this because I knew that he would do something desperate.

I don't know how but he got some hot soup or some hot tea for me to drink and he pushed me out to the assembly place. He went up to the kapo and told him, "My best friend can't make it anymore. Don't take him to the quarry. I'll do double the work, but don't take him." The kapo was a little bit humane and he let me stay.

"Try to stay busy," Jakob warned me. "Otherwise I don't know how you'll be able to stay in the barracks."

Soon after he left, the kapos came around. I told them I couldn't work in the quarry anymore. They could kill me, I said, but why not give me some work here instead. One of the kapos said to the other in German, "Let him clean up here. Make him be useful." I started cleaning and the day passed. I didn't know if they forgot about me. I wasn't going to question it. They didn't give me any food, but I really didn't care. I felt like a zombie.

When Jakob came back, he shared his soup with me, which wasn't easy for him after working hard all day. We decided that it was impossible for either of us to go back to the quarry because we were not going to come out alive. Fortunately, at the same time that we made that decision, they assembled everybody who had been in Auschwitz in a transport to go to Melk concentration camp. We said to each other, "We don't care where we're going." I knew I wouldn't survive at Mauthausen another day because I was feeling so dizzy.

Melk was a city not far from Mauthausen, in Upper Austria. It's maybe an hour from Linz and a couple of hours from Salzburg. The Germans were hiding V-2 and V-3 rockets in the mountains and they built the ammunition factories for the war effort there so the Allied air force wouldn't be able to find them and bomb them. Some of the factories were already built, but they needed more space and so they needed more labour.

A few thousand of us were transported to Melk concentration camp by trucks and then by train. They put us in barracks, gave us some hot soup and put us to work building tunnels in the mountains. It wasn't easy but it wasn't as bad as in the quarry. At least it was liveable, although the work was very dangerous. We blasted tunnels in the mountains with dynamite and shovelled the earth to be taken out, first by wheelbarrows and then by rail carts. It was already February and I didn't feel as cold as before. The sun was shining. And they gave us hot coffee in the morning with a piece of bread.

We worked in three shifts, day and night. Naturally, as newcomers, we were given the most dangerous part of the labour – dynamiting. There was no way that you could really protect yourself and many didn't survive the work. But we were rather lucky at that time because the Soviets were advancing. The front was coming closer and by now I was hearing rumours that Melk concentration camp was going to be dissolved.

The most dangerous thing in Melk was the main kapo. They called him the Gypsy kapo and it seemed that he liked killing people. Perhaps he wanted to show the Nazis that he could do a better job at cruelty than they did. Mind you, he didn't only pick on Jews. He targeted all the prisoners. He killed people while the German guards laughed and clapped. He carried a big club like a baseball bat. If he didn't like a person, he hit him on the head and split his head right in half.

At Melk, however, at least there was a hospital and it wasn't only for killing people or experimenting on them, like it was in Auschwitz. Something remarkable happened to me in Melk. One day, I felt that I couldn't walk any more. I was feverish, but that was common when we were starving. Fever, headaches and dizziness were a daily routine. But I noticed that my feet were swollen, especially my two big toes. I started limping and it slowed me down when we walked to work. I took off my shoes and my socks fell apart. The nails on my toes were gone. My feet were both bleeding and raw, and white from the cold. I showed this to Jakob. When he saw my feet he was afraid I wouldn't be able to walk to work. From Melk it was maybe an hour or two walk to get to the tunnels where we worked.

I told Jakob to take me to the hospital. He and a couple of other men took me there, Jakob knocked on the door and they left me there while they went back to work. They were afraid if they stood around they would be shot. We all said our goodbyes – we had never seen anybody return from a hospital in Auschwitz, so we all felt that we might never see each other again. I couldn't even stand. I sat on a rock. Finally the door opened and a man in a doctor's white coat came out.

He asked me in German, "What happened to you?" I tried to stand up, but I couldn't. I showed him my toes and said to him, "I know what hospitals are. Just give me a little bit of salve and a bandage. I'll take care of it myself."

Instead, he sent for a stretcher and told two inmates who worked in the hospital to take my number and find me a bed. I figured I had to take the risk and tell him that I was okay and wanted to get back to the barracks. After Auschwitz, I was afraid of hospitals. He came closer to me and whispered, "Don't worry. I'm a Jew." I looked at him and he nodded his head. He took me by the arm, put me on a bed and bandaged my feet. He was pretending to be a Christian, passing as a perfect German.

I was in the hospital for a few days. He told me his name was Klaus. "Dr. Klaus?" I asked. "Nein, nein" he answered. He was only partially trained as a doctor, but the camp administration had made him a full doctor in this hospital. He helped me to recuperate. After we were liberated, I met him again in Gmunden and we became friends. I have photos of him and I also helped organize his wedding. Later on, I helped him out financially and gave him a good recommendation to the American consul, which helped him go to the United States.

We must have been in Melk two weeks or so when a high-ranking German SS officer came into the barracks and he called out in German, "Who is a *Schneider*? Is anybody here a tailor?"

Jakob spoke up, "I am a *Schneider*."

"Okay, come with me." The SS man led Jakob out and showed him a large men's wool coat with a fur collar and fur lining. The German told Jakob it was too big for him – probably, he added, because it had belonged to a very fat, rich Jew. This officer was skinny and tall. He asked Jakob if he could fix the coat to fit him. Jakob agreed right away. He was thinking that it would be one way to get out of the hard work in the tunnels.

"I want this in three days," the German said.

Jakob wasn't born yesterday. He said, "I'm very weak, I can't work that fast." And he was weak, but he couldn't say he was too weak to do it.

Obviously the SS officer didn't care. He just wanted the job done. He said, "I'll give you some bread now. Just fix it." A couple of hours later, Jakob came in with a nice portion of bread.

As we ate the bread I asked Jakob if he couldn't drag it out, making the work last as long as possible. He said, "I can do it in three hours if I want to, but I told him three days and for those three days we're going to get bread and soup. And on top of that, I'm not going to work."

So Jakob stayed in the barracks. He took off the sleeves and made them shorter. When he took off one sleeve, he found a whole bag of diamonds sewn inside the lining. When I came back from work I saw Jakob's face. I had never seen a smile on his face quite like that.

"Come here, take a look," he told me. He took out the bag of diamonds, very little ones. There must have been a couple hundred of them. I had never seen a diamond in my life, or if I had, I didn't know what it was. Thanks to these diamonds we both survived. He took a diamond to the kitchen and traded it for bread and a piece of salami. We hadn't had a piece of salami for such a long time. And the cook also gave us some soup.

In this way, we survived until they closed Melk concentration camp in early April. The weather was nice and warm. The Soviet army was already in Vienna and American forces were in Germany and advancing through Italy. The Germans took us to the town and put us all on a boat. We thought they were going to drown us. Instead, they took us by boat along the Danube River to Linz, one group at a time. At Linz, we weren't given anything to eat. We waited there while the boat went back and forth from Melk to Linz. Once they had assembled close to 10,000 of us, they marched us from Linz to Ebensee, which would end up being the last camp we were in. By car it would take two or three hours to go from Linz to this camp. It was high up in the big mountains that run through Austria and I still don't know how I made it there. Quite a few didn't. A few thousand people walked all the way there. I can even remember the names of the cities we passed from Linz: Lambach, Wels, Gmunden and Ebensee. They called the area Salzkammergut, which is a province in Upper Austria, the capital of which is Salzburg.

The SS guards weren't accompanying us any longer and we didn't see any more of them until we reached Ebensee; there were only German soldiers on the march and they weren't quite as ruthless, so we didn't have to march quickly. They didn't shoot anyone who fell behind. Still, it was a very tough march. Jakob and I made sure we weren't lagging behind. By the time we got to Ebensee, I was nearly unconscious because I was so dehydrated. I could hardly make it to the water pump once we got to the camp, but I somehow managed. Probably Jakob helped me. I drank, put my head under the water and started feeling better.

In Ebensee, you could say we went from the frying pan into the fire. This concentration camp was built for five or six thousand people. In the end, there were about 18,000 of us there. It was hard to find a place to sleep. Ebensee was constructed for the same reason as Melk, to build and store ammunition for the war. Before us, Italian and Soviet POWs had been held there. Ebensee was a gruesome camp. I never met the commander of Ebensee, but from what I was told by other inmates, his favourite pastime was to sic his killer dog on prisoners. People heard the screams from prisoners as the dog ran after them. After we were liberated, the Americans found one of the commandants of the Mauthausen subcamps in the mountains and arrested him, but the commander of Ebensee eluded capture until the early 1970s.

Once again, there was lots of work and no food. Ebensee didn't have large enough kitchens to cook for so many people and they didn't have supplies. Food was simply a commodity that barely existed anymore. This was the last corner of the German Reich. Everybody

– the Soviets, the Americans, the British – was closing in on them. Jakob and I started to work blasting dynamite inside tunnels to make storage space in the mountain. Then, with wheelbarrows, we had to remove the rubble. A group of a hundred people went in and half of us came out alive, covered with sand and stones. Everything had to be done too quickly and some were crushed when a roof caved in. They needed new places for the rockets. Tunnels were collapsing. Explosives were blowing up prematurely. Every day they had to remove dead bodies because they were in such a rush that there were no safety precautions. We worked there day and night, night and day. The guards were watching with guns, ordering us to move faster.

Jakob tried to find a way to get us out of there. The end of the war was near and we had made it too far to be killed in that hell hole. Jakob saw there were lots of people working outside, repairing things, delivering dynamite and all kinds of other tasks, so he took a chance and went to the kapo to offer him a bribe. He said, "Here are a couple of diamonds from me and my friend. You'll get even more if you give us another job around here instead of in the tunnels."

The kapo took the diamonds and told his foreman to assign us to another task, clearing out the tool shack. We were saved. Jakob and I would never have survived inside the tunnels. Jakob also bribed a cook with another few diamonds and we got a little extra soup. We didn't get beaten up any more, either – all because of those diamonds.

But the day came when they simply did not have any food for us at all. The supply vehicles couldn't get through because the Allies were blocking the roads, so we couldn't even buy soup with the diamonds. The Germans didn't have food for their own people. We were still getting coffee, or something hot and black anyway, but our hunger became so terrible that we were crushing the limestone that came out of the tunnels and putting it in our coffee to make it a little bit thicker. In all of Ebensee, the grass was gone – eaten. All the trees were stripped of bark. The tar was gone from the roofs. That was our diet for the last ten days.

It got worse. The Allied Forces began bombing the railways. Near the end of April, almost our last days at Ebensee, the Germans asked for volunteers to work at repairing the tracks. They could have forced us to go if they wanted to, but they asked for volunteers. A truck with a loudspeaker came around one morning, gathering people to work outside the camp at the railroad station. Generally, a veteran does not volunteer, not in a camp, but there was no food and I thought there might be something to steal around the station. So I volunteered. I went with the trucks and I worked the whole night, taking away the broken train rails and repairing broken buildings. Because this station was a place where many railroad tracks crossed, it was a good target for the Allies.

On the very first day, I had a bit of luck. I found a sack of peas and I smuggled it back to camp. I put the peas in two cups of coffee with the limestone and I gave one to Jakob. "Oh, this is good," he said. Hot black water with soft rocks and a little bit of peas. It was a banquet.

I volunteered again to go to the station and whenever I had a chance, I stole some food from the warehouses around there or from the trains. I could have gotten shot for it, but I didn't care anymore. Sometimes I didn't get anything, but most of the time there were *Magazines* to loot and a lot of the time the townspeople gave me something. The work there continued, because the station was constantly bombed.

Suddenly, the trips to work at the station stopped. Either the Allies stopped bombing or the Germans were afraid to leave the compound because on our last trip to the station, the airplanes overhead had strafed us. There had been five or six of us going at a time and an SS officer guarding us. If not, we would have escaped. They didn't have enough guards now because a lot of the SS were running away themselves. They heard that Linz was gone. Mauthausen was gone. Vienna was already under Soviet occupation.

Finally, we knew that the end was near. A few guys were brave enough to kill that Gypsy kapo from Melk who had come with us to

Ebensee. It happened in my barracks, where he was trying to hide. These guys took some planks and they beat him until there was nothing left of him. I saw this and I said to myself, "Now the end is really here." No Germans were coming to protect him.

We were no longer going to work and there were fewer and fewer Germans around. Two or three days before the Americans arrived, the commander of Ebensee got his lackeys together. They put us all in the *Appellplatz*, the square where we assembled for work. He made a speech on the loudspeaker, "Well, *Kameraden*...[comrades]." All of a sudden we were *Kameraden*. He said, "*Kameraden*, those American devils are bombing everybody and they're going to bomb us pretty soon. Let's all go inside the tunnels where we'll be safe."

Nobody moved. We knew that there was dynamite in front of the entrance to the tunnels. The Germans were so spoiled and lazy that they didn't do any manual labour. They made our people bring dynamite up to the entrances. If they had brought the dynamite themselves, we might not have known about it. Maybe we would have gone, but we started thinking, "Why would they put dynamite at the entrance instead of down in the tunnels where it's used? And, now he's telling us to go into the mountain." So we put two and two together and it came to: "They want to blow us up." There were about 18,000 of us with SS all around and we weren't moving. He said, "Didn't I tell you to go inside the mountain?" We still didn't move. He said, "Well, I'm giving you three minutes." The three minutes passed. Nothing. He started yelling. We still didn't budge.

That was the first time we had defied the Germans and their machineguns. They didn't want to shoot us with the American soldiers so close by. The commander and other SS officers had no choice. They brought in veteran soldiers with old rifles who were part of a civilian militia, the German People's Army, or *Volkssturm*, to guard us until the Americans came. Then they took their cars and motorcycles and took off into the mountains.

Jakob and I were in Ebensee with a group of men that included a pair of twins approximately my age, Polish Jews. We knew them from Auschwitz. Despite being twins, they had managed to avoid Dr. Mengele. We always grouped together and made sure that wherever we went, we stayed together and looked out for each other. Sometimes if one guy got in trouble, the others could help him.

Now we were stuck in Ebensee with no food. I don't know how long we hadn't eaten because my head was buzzing. I hardly knew where I was or what I was doing. After all we'd been through, we were going to drop dead from starvation. We couldn't even get the limestone from the tunnels because we weren't going out to work anymore.

Sometimes we thought we could smell food when we went by a certain area of the camp. We thought, "How could there be a smell of food around here?"

Then we saw a Russian guy eating a piece of meat. We asked him, "Where did you get it?"

He said, "Well, there's lots of bodies lying around."

Some of them were making a business by cooking the meat of the dead people over a fire and trading it. He was ready to give us a piece but it was too horrifying. We moved away, although we were so hungry that it wasn't that easy to resist. That's how desperate we were in Ebensee. I want you to know that I never did eat it, but I did think about it.

A few days before we were liberated, one of the twins, Moishe, disappeared. He probably went to look for food. His brother, Yankel, was frantic and he yelled to us to help find him. We searched and called out, "Moishe!" but we couldn't find him. I offered to look once more around the barracks. It was getting dark and there was no longer any electricity. Jakob warned me, "Don't go too far away. If you collapse somewhere I won't be able to find you."

At Ebensee, there was a special *Kommando* whose job was finding bodies and bringing them to the crematorium in carts. It wasn't a gas chamber. Nobody was gassed in Ebensee. It was just a crematorium to burn the bodies of inmates who died and it wasn't even working because the people in the *Kommando* were too weak to lift the corpses into the furnace. The bodies were just piled up on the grounds of the crematorium. As I was searching, I passed a heap of bodies. All of a sudden I thought I heard my name coming from the corpses. I shuddered. The dead were calling my name. But I heard it again. This time I recognized the voice.

I said, "Moishe?" and he started groaning.

Moishe was lying in the middle of a pile of bodies. He must have passed out and while he was lying where he fell, the people who dragged the bodies to the crematorium probably thought he was dead and they took him. When he woke up he was too weak to lift himself out of the corpses. He was calling out, but the crematorium was too far away from the barracks for us to hear him. When he saw me, he called, "Felix, it's me. It's me." So I asked him a stupid question, which they laughed at me about later. I asked him, "What are you doing here?"

"Felix," he said, "help me. I can't get out."

I grabbed his arm and started pulling him. His arm was like a piece of stick. He screamed with pain, "You're pulling my arm off!"

I couldn't get him out. I didn't have the strength to move the bodies. I was too weak and too tired and I didn't know what to do. I was starting to get faint. I called out the names of the other guys to come help me and finally they heard me and came running. I was so out of breath from yelling I could only point to the pile of bodies. They still couldn't understand what I was talking about. It wasn't easy to get the picture right away. All the bodies looked the same. They were skeletons. When they finally caught on, they took off the corpses from on top and pulled him out. He was almost dead. We revived him and he survived. I was flabbergasted that he could still survive from that. Both Yankel and Moishe survived and, in fact, I later went to Moishe's wedding. Unfortunately, I lost track of the twins later, although Jakob and I stuck together.

Liberation

On the morning of May 5 the few old soldiers who were guarding us yelled in German, "Leave if you want to go. You're all free." Nobody stirred because we thought it was another trick. They were shouting, "The Americans are in the next town. They're coming up here." We still didn't budge. First the SS tried to fool us with dynamite and now maybe these old men with guns were trying to trick us. We were sure that if we moved they would gun us down and use the excuse that we were attacking the old soldiers. We just lay on the ground. It was nice, warm and sunny outside.

After awhile, however, Jakob and I felt secure enough to walk out of the camp for a bit. By the next day, even the old soldiers were gone. When we heard the sound of the tanks coming, we said to ourselves, "Oh, now there you are. The Germans are back with tanks. See, it was all a trick." So the few hundred guys who were lying in the big *Appellplatz* moved back to hide in the barracks in case the Germans were returning to kill us. These tanks, however, came right through the gate. We'd never seen this before because when the German tanks arrived, they always stopped at the barrier to salute the guards, who opened the gates for them. Now we saw three green military tanks roll up. The drivers weren't saluting. They weren't waiting. Nobody opened the gates for them. They came right through, breaking the barrier. They stopped in the middle of the camp but they didn't see any people because we were hiding. They got out of the tanks and took out a map to check if they were in the right place. Someone who was close enough to see the insignia on the tank called out in Polish, "Americans!" It was the 80th Infantry Division of the 3rd US Army.

Can you imagine what happened then? I don't know where the energy came from, but suddenly we weren't weak anymore. Thousands of us miraculously found the energy to make a rush for the three tanks. I hadn't even been able to walk two minutes before, but now I leapt up and ran toward the tanks. When those few soldiers saw such a mob, they jumped back into the tank and closed the turret. They were afraid of us. They didn't know what we were going to do.

We banged on the tanks, yelling, "Americans!" That's the only word we knew in English. We were thumping on the tanks, yelling and shouting, "Americans! Americans! Americans!" Finally, they opened up and started talking to us. They saw they were in the right place. They saw how emaciated we were, so they threw out their K-rations to us. Everybody tried to grab them. All I managed to get my hands on was a piece of cellophane paper. I put this scrap of wrapping to my nose and smelled the food. I put it in my mouth, like I was eating food. I felt food. Just the smell of the food was enough to revive me.

The Americans had radios and contacted their commander, who was about twenty kilometres away, asking him to hold back the army and send in the Red Cross doctors. It took a couple of hours for the ambulances to arrive.

Jakob and I saw that we really were free and we could leave the camp, so we did the worst thing we could have done – we ran to a farm and asked if we could have some food. They didn't have much but they were more afraid than anything else when they saw who was knocking at the door. They gave us whatever they had. They took us to the place where they kept potatoes for the pigs and we ate just like the pigs. We shovelled down all the potatoes. Then we went to another farm and another farm until we felt that we couldn't eat any more, but our minds still wanted it. I immediately felt the food go right through me.

That's what hunger does to you. We kept eating and the food was passing right through us. I couldn't stop and I fainted. Jakob had diarrhea too, but not as bad. He dragged me back to the camp. We lay on the ground and we were happy, looking up at the stars. A few hours later, when it started getting dark, we got hungry again. We went out and found more food. The second time when we got diarrhea, we couldn't make it back to the camp. I don't know who helped us, but I think it was an American.

The Austrian police and doctors came to the camp from the town of Ebensee. A few thousand people had the same problem that we had. We were laid out on the field and they gave us some medicine. I was unconscious again and I remember waking up feeling that somebody was pouring cement into my mouth. I saw an American doctor and a nurse in white with helpers who spoke a little bit of German. I asked, "Why did they pour cement in me?" They laughed and said, "It's medication, but it tastes like cement." That stuff saved me. It settled my stomach and after a few days I felt better.

Our liberators couldn't do too much because they weren't ready for the multitude of people. They didn't have regular food, just soup. We craved solid food. It felt as though we didn't care if we were going to die eating, as long as we got to eat. After I got better they tried to keep me from running out of the camp for more food. But Jakob and I still went out again, straight from the makeshift hospital. Nobody could really stop us. Approximately five thousand of us got diarrhea and close to a thousand of us died from it. The doctors just didn't have the facilities to care for us; they only had a few supplies in case the soldiers got sick.

Once Jakob and I felt better, we wondered what we were going to do. We couldn't stay in the camp. We got together with some of the other men and decided we would try to get back to Poland. The only problem was that we didn't know how we would get there. There was no transportation. We talked to an American who said, "If you guys can walk to Gmunden, which is about thirty kilometres away, that's where our headquarters are." He explained that maybe they could put us in touch with an organization that could help us. So we started walking.

We were still wearing our striped uniforms as we walked down the highway. We just wanted to get to the station and take a train to go home. We wanted to find our families. We asked some locals where the train station was and they told us that it was a little bit farther down the road. We walked about ten kilometres. Then we sat down on the edge of the highway to rest.

Two American soldiers came by in a jeep and stopped. They asked us where we were going, in English. We didn't understand. We said in Yiddish that we wanted to go home. One soldier was an American Jew and he could speak a little bit of Yiddish. He said, "Where are you going? Would you like a lift?" We told him that we had just come from the camp and were headed to the train station. The officer offered to take us there. We piled into the jeep, sitting one on top of the other.

Apparently the driver said to the Jewish soldier, "These guys look half-starved. Before we take them to the station, why don't we take them to our kitchen and feed them?" They knew it wasn't going to be easy for us to get food until we got to the train station. The Jewish solider asked us, "Would you like to eat something before you go home?"

Eat? Of course we'd like to eat!

They took us to their base in Gmunden and led us to a makeshift military kitchen, which had previously been a nightclub. Gmunden was about an hour away from both Salzburg and Linz, approximately in the middle of the northern part of Austria. It's a tourist town now.

The soldiers gave us food and drinks. The Jewish soldier told us to eat and rest a little bit and then they would drive us to the station. We ate and ate and ate. It wasn't food like the farmers had given us. There was white bread with salami, cheese and such juicy food that it made us feel like we were on another planet.

When we were done, there was a little bit of a mess that the soldiers had left and a little mess from us. We offered to clean up the place for them before we left. The Jewish soldier thought this was a great idea and told us that he would give us something for the road in exchange. While we were cleaning, one of the officers came by and wanted to know what we were doing. When the soldiers explained why we were there, he said, "How about keeping these fellows here? We'll give them food and they can clean for us." At that time, the Americans were not supposed to fraternize with the Austrian population, so they couldn't hire help. What American soldier would want to clean? It was enough they had to cook for themselves. When the soldiers told us we could eat as much as we'd like, we readily agreed to work for them.

I don't know exactly how much I weighed then, maybe seventy or eighty pounds. This idea was heavenly! We'd have cleaned the whole city if they'd asked us to. So we remained in Gmunden where the Americans were stationed. A few days turned into four years. I met my wife and got married there and my eldest daughter was born there.

Before I met my wife, I returned to Poland to see if I could find anyone from my family or from my friends' families. The other men chose me to go because I was the youngest in the group. I went to Lodz in October 1945 and put my name down in the Jewish Committee offices and checked around. I went to the neighbourhood where I was born, but nobody had seen my family there. I went to the neighbours, but they were different people already. When I went to the place where I had lived, the woman there said, "I was given this apartment by the government."

"I don't want to take it away from you," I assured her. "I just want to know if you have seen anyone from my family."

"No, no," she said.

I went to another couple of cities where my friends came from to look for their relatives, but there was nothing. There weren't any re-cords or news about any of them. When I saw what the situation was, I started making my way back to Gmunden. But by then, the political situation made it more difficult than when I had come. With the help of an underground organization called Bricha, I smuggled myself out of Poland, which was under Soviet control, through Germany to Berlin and back to the Americans in Austria.

~

When life started getting back to normal after the war was over, the Americans didn't need the field kitchen any more. They could eat in hotels. Nevertheless, their base was big and they decided to make it into a nightclub. They hired us to run it and we worked day and night for the same wages: food.

A few months after we were liberated some Jews from British Mandate Palestine came looking for volunteers to help fight in the army they were forming there. At that time the Jewish population of pre-state Israel was more than half a million and there were about 400 times that many Arabs in the surrounding territories. The Jews wanted to have a country but they needed volunteers. One day a man came to the club and asked us if we wanted to go to Palestine. Then he asked, "Who is Felix?" They pointed me out to him. He said, "I heard that you're a specialist in explosives." Somebody had told him that I was involved in the uprising in Auschwitz. I tried to explain to him that I had done some smuggling for the Underground, but I wasn't a specialist in any kind of ammunition. He wouldn't take no for an answer. I considered going with him because I felt homeless. But that was before I met my wife who said, "If you want to go to Israel, you go by yourself."

At the nightclub, the American soldiers would come to eat and drink booze, which was brought in from the Post Exchange (PX). Alcohol was rationed and the soldiers had ration cards. I got to know some of them a little bit and I learned a few words in English – not words I'd use when I talk to my wife or my kids, but a few words. The American soldiers saw the way we were dressed – we still wore our striped uniforms from the camp – and they didn't like it. They brought us working clothes – plain American uniforms – and they even brought me a hat and a pair of gloves.

I figured that if I could get a bottle of liquor, I could give it to the men who were so nice to me. I didn't want to do any business; I just wanted to give them a gift to thank them. Everybody was out to make a deal in those days, but I was very naive. What happened next was all by accident. A soldier from the PX gave me a bottle as a gift because I had helped him bring in a case of liquor. I stashed it away and when I saw one of the men who had been sympathetic to me, I took out the bottle and gave it to him. He took it and took out ten dollars in American military money, which they called scrip and gave it to me. I intended the booze as a gift, but he was happy to pay to get some extra booze under the counter.

I took the scrip and I went to some friends in Gmunden who were jewellers. They were from a *Kommando* in a camp that worked in counterfeiting American dollars and British pounds. I asked them if they'd exchange the scrip for me for what it was worth. They said it was worth between seven and ten dollars in the market, but they would only give me seven dollars in US currency. I took the money and when I saw the soldier from the PX again, I took out five dollars to give to him. I did this because I wanted to show him that I knew what five dollars was. I said, "Five. Five." He misunderstood and thought I wanted five bottles because he had given me one bottle before. Five dollars was a lot to him. He nodded and he took the five dollars and brought me five bottles. It didn't cost him anything. He was just swiping it from the PX.

I took the five bottles back to the nightclub. All of a sudden I now had five bottles and I didn't know what to do with them. I put them away and tried to get rid of them very quickly. I was afraid that if anybody saw these bottles, they'd think I'd stolen them. I worried that

I would lose my job. I sold the five bottles to the soldiers I knew and soon they were bringing me more money. For those five bottles I got a hundred dollars in scrip. They had asked me how much and I didn't know how to say the numbers in English, but they gave me twenty for each bottle.

I went back to my friends, the jewellers, with a hundred military dollars. They said, "We can give you fifty American dollars now and we'll give you another ten or twenty dollars later on. We haven't got so much around."

I took the money and, when there was another delivery, I took out all the money I had and I showed it to the soldier. I didn't know how much to give him because I didn't know the prices. He could be arrested if he got caught selling the booze anyway. If I gave him fifty dollars, that would be ten dollars a bottle, lots of money. But I was already thinking of something else besides liquor: chocolate and American cigarettes. You could make any kind of a deal for American cigarettes back then. So I asked him, "Chocolate? Cigarettes?" I knew those words already. He looked at me and he shook his head, but he took the money. It wasn't so easy. He had to steal the goods.

When I gave him fifty dollars, he said, "Too much." I didn't know what he meant but that's what it sounded like. He handed a couple of bills back to me.

I said, "No, no. That's for you." He wasn't a fool; he put the money in his pocket. He was glad to get American dollars because the soldiers couldn't use military scrip to buy anything in the city. They couldn't take a girl to a hotel or a restaurant with military money, so they needed dollars.

The next time, the solider brought out a case of French cognac and a carton of cigarettes. He asked me how much I could take. I could have had a whole case of fifty cartons, but I had no place to store it. I took three cartons and some chocolate into the nightclub. That was tricky. There were other soldiers around and there was the manager of the club. Everybody saw me with it, but they didn't know where it was going. Once I found a place to hide everything, I had a whole shelf of chocolate, booze and cigarettes. I showed it to Jakob.

"Where did you get this? Did you steal it?" Jakob asked. "They'll probably throw us out or shoot us."

I told him the story. He called over our other friends and we all discussed it. "Don't yell at Felix," they told Jakob. "He has something here." That was around the middle of 1946 and it was the beginning of our black-marketeering.

I became the main black marketeer because I started it. I was the one who had the connection to the Americans and I was the one who brought in the goods. Jakob was the one who sold the alcohol to the soldiers. Then, somebody had to go and exchange the money. I had more military money to change for American dollars, but the jewellers didn't have that much cash on hand. They had just opened a store. They were survivors like me. I asked them where to go and they told me to try Linz, where there was the biggest DP (displaced persons) camp in Austria, called Bindermichl.

I went to Linz by train, carrying the scrip. The people in the DP camp could take it to well-connected Americans and exchange it for 50 per cent. The Americans knew where to exchange it for 80 per cent. Everyone was making money; it felt as though they were just waiting for me to arrive.

The trip took half a day each way by train. We started working in the club at four o'clock in the afternoon and we finished cleaning up sometime in the morning. I would leave for Linz after that.

Everything was going very nice and smoothly, maybe too smoothly, until I said to Jakob, "This isn't fast enough. Something has to be done."

Jakob liked it the way it was.

I said, "I can't go to Linz like this every day. It takes half a day. I have to go there, see where to get the best price and then I have to get to the station and come back. And then I have to work at night in the club."

"What do you want to do instead?" Jakob asked.

I told him that we needed a motorcycle or a car. I didn't know how to drive a car, but I figured if I knew how to ride a bicycle, I could manage a motorcycle. We went to a gas station close by. It was owned by an American who had a German working for him. He told us that once in a while they had an old car or an old motorcycle for sale. We told him if he got a decent motorcycle he should let us know. A few days later the garage owner came around with a motorcycle.

"What do you want for it?" I asked.

"Don't give me any money," he said. "I need other things that you've got to sell."

"A bottle of whiskey?" I offered.

"Yeah, maybe. Maybe two bottles."

I said, "Okay, two bottles."

Then he said, "And how about a pack of cigarettes?" I knew what he was going to say next. "Can you make it a carton?"

So I brought out two bottles and a carton of cigarettes. But first I made him promise to teach me how to ride the motorcycle. When I finished my shift I went with Jakob and the German assistant taught us to ride. I started riding but I couldn't get it right away. It took me a couple of days. There was one thing that I never could remember. I couldn't understand why when the motorcycle stopped, it didn't fall down. All the rider does is put his foot down, but I didn't see that. Eventually I got it.

I went to Bindermichl by motorcycle with the scrip and came back with American money. I was making a lot of money, so I got greedy. Sometimes it doesn't pay to be so greedy, but then again, if I hadn't been so greedy, I wouldn't have met my wife, so everything is connected.

Going to Linz once a day was not enough for me anymore; I began to go twice a day. Going to Linz from Gmunden was about 80 kilometres. I also worked at the nightclub in the evening. I didn't have time to sleep enough and it took a toll on me. One day, when I had driven for too long, I had an accident. I ran into a big truck filled with American soldiers. My leg was broken in three places and my left arm was broken; I was in very bad shape. I was wearing an American uniform because those were the only clothes I had. The guys in the truck thought I was an American, but then they saw I didn't have a dog tag. Right away they got suspicious. Then they saw the tattooed number on my broken arm.

They took me to a military hospital and the nurses there told them, "We can't take him here. You have to take him to a private hospital." So they took me to a private hospital, where the doctors admitted me. I was unconscious from the pain and loss of blood.

Jakob got in touch with the doctor in charge of my treatment, who told him that my leg was infected and that he was going to have to amputate it. Jakob said, "Before you take off any legs, I want to have a talk with you." Jakob came into the hospital with a bag full of liquor, chocolate and also a revolver. He put this on the table in the doctor's office and he told the doctor, "All this is for you if you don't take off his leg. If you cure him, there'll be much more to come. But if you take off his leg, this gun you see here has a bullet for your head."

The doctor said, "I cannot help. You can threaten me as much as you want. He's got an infection in his leg. I have to take it off or else he's going to die."

"So what's the alternative?" Jakob asked.

"Penicillin."

"Penicillin?" Jakob said, "I don't know what that is." Penicillin, an antibiotic, was only just starting to be used in the 1940s.

The doctor told him that the private hospital didn't have penicillin. Only the American army had it. Mostly they kept it for soldiers who got venereal diseases. Jakob finally found out where he could get penicillin, but it cost thirty-five American dollars on the black market for one shot and the suppliers had to go to Vienna to get it. We had already accumulated close to a thousand dollars. He spent all the money for me to get the penicillin and he saved my leg. He saved me.

I was a mess in the hospital for almost a year. While I was re-cuperating, Yankel, the brother of Moishe, whom we had saved in Ebensee, dropped in. It was sheer coincidence that he had shown up in Gmunden. Good karma and more twists of fate followed from that visit, because that's how I eventually met my future wife, Regina, who had recently returned from the Soviet Union.

Many Polish Jewish families fled to the Soviet Union at the be-ginning of the war. The Soviet administration sent some of them to labour camps in Siberia, but after the war the Soviet government didn't want the Polish Jews there anymore. They had enough mouths of their own to feed. They repatriated them back to Poland, but they didn't get a very good reception in Poland either. There were even some pogroms against the Jews when they returned.

Among the people coming back from the Soviet Union was my future wife and her family. They had returned home to Poland but then fled when the Polish Communist government took over and they headed for the American Zone in Austria. They arrived with a group of people, including the twin brothers, who had also gone to Poland and come back when they experienced all the antisemi-tism there. They all ended up in Ebensee, which had been turned into a DP camp. An organization called the United Nations Relief and Rehabilitation Administration (UNRRA) provided medical care and food and later helped some DPs immigrate to North America.

Yankel told me that Moishe had fallen in love with a girl in the camp and was about to get married. This girl was best friends with my future wife, who was going to be her bridesmaid. As they were preparing the wedding, Moishe had said to his brother, "Look, I don't know if we have enough food. The whole camp is going to be at the wedding. Can you go to Gmunden and see if you can buy some things there?"

Yankel came to Gmunden and saw the club. He didn't realize that the club was connected to the American military, so he thought maybe he could buy some food inside. He came into the club and saw

Jakob and the other guys from the camp. He was so happy, kissing and hugging them. Then he looked around and said, "Jakob, where is Felix? Did Felix survive?"

"Felix had an accident," Jakob replied. "He's in the hospital." He then told them the story.

"When I tell Moishe that I found Jakob, he's going to be very happy, although he won't be happy that Felix is in the hospital."

Yankel came to visit me in the hospital and told me that Moishe was getting married soon. "You know he'll want you at the wedding," he said.

It was already winter, getting colder. How could I go to a wedding? I was in a hospital with an arm and a leg in casts. But these were survivors; I couldn't say no to them. None of us ever gave up so easily. So soon after, Yankel got together with Jakob and with another few fellows from our group and they all went to the hospital. They bribed a few nurses so they could smuggle me out by securing me to the bed, opening the window and lowering me down with ropes. They had hired an American jeep and driver and they put me in the back, bed and all, and started driving up to Ebensee.

The camp was right on the mountain. Because they were so excited, they forgot about the steep roads and the snow and ice. The jeep couldn't make it. They couldn't pull the bed up the mountain, even though it was on wheels. They went to a farm and asked the farmer to rent them a sleigh for ten dollars. For the farmer, ten dollars in 1946 was a lot of money. They laughed and said, "We'll give you the bed, too." So they tied me onto the sleigh and pulled me the rest of the way.

Unfortunately, just before they got to the camp, I slid off the sleigh and the cast on my leg broke. They sort of put me back together, but the cast moved and I was in excruciating pain. I was sweating. Moishe said he wouldn't get married if I wasn't there. I didn't want to spoil the wedding so I didn't say anything, but I was pale and felt faint. When we came up to the groom's barracks, one of the guys said, "Hey, Felix, are you okay?"

I said, "Of course I'm okay. When is the wedding?" I just wanted to get it over with. I wanted to go back to the hospital.

They got a kind of nurse to look at me. She guessed that my leg moved when the cast broke and her and my friends tried to tie the cast up with strings, ties, belts, whatever they had. It was a little better, maybe because it didn't move anymore, but I was still in pain.

All this took time. Meanwhile, the bride was getting impatient and wondering where Moishe was. The wedding was supposed to be inside the barracks, but the whole camp wanted to come to it so they held it outside and everybody was freezing cold. The bride asked her best friend, Regina, "Can you go to the barracks and see if the groom is still alive? What's the matter with him?"

She found us and saw my friends trying to take care of me. She said that the whole camp was waiting for the wedding. "What's the matter with you guys? We're freezing and you're here playing around with a guy on a bed with ropes." This was my future wife, Regina. Everything is connected. Like I said, karma. Moishe said, "Go back and explain to them that this man saved my life once. If he is not going to be at the wedding, I'm not going to be at the wedding."

She went back and told everybody, "He'll be here any minute."

Finally they secured me back on the sleigh and dragged me out to the wedding. Everybody drank, made toasts and had something to eat.

After the wedding, they took me back to the hospital. It took all night because the driver of the jeep wouldn't stay waiting for us in the freezing cold and he had left. I don't even remember how we got back because I was in such horrible pain and I had a fever. They were wiping the sweat from my face. From this episode, I lost three months of healing and had to begin all over again.

When I got a little better, I went to Ebensee by train or by hitching a ride and reconnected with Regina. We started dating, which wasn't easy for me. She was a beautiful girl and I was a cripple in a cast. She also told me that she wasn't ready to marry. She wasn't as crazy about me as I was for her. Also, her parents didn't want her to see me; at that time a lot of people felt uncomfortable around survivors from the camps. But I overcame all these things. I overcame my cast and I overcame her parents. And a lot of guys wanted to date her. One competitor was an American officer with whom I did business. When he found out that she liked me better, I lost all contact with him. Winning her wasn't an easy task and to be honest, I still don't know how I did it.

Ebensee soon closed and they took all the displaced persons near Salzburg to a DP camp called Hallein. It was half a day away by train, but at least I could still see Regina, so it was better than nothing. I went there and sometimes Regina came to Gmunden with one of her family members as chaperone.

We were married on June 16, 1947 and our first daughter, Esther, was born on November 14, 1947, in Gmunden. Then, with the assistance of the International Refugee Organization, we came to Halifax in April 1949 and then travelled to Toronto. I had applied to come to Canada as a furrier. Regina's parents had come to Toronto the year before, which really helped our application and also helped us settle in our new country. People who came to Canada or America and had nobody struggled harder than we did.

In Toronto I worked at various jobs until I met a fellow who wanted to go into business with me. My very first business was a billiards hall because I saw that these places were always busy. After that I began a business in coin-operated washing machines. Later, I was involved in construction and machines and appliances and I made a decent living. Time passed and I established myself in the community. I prospered and I bought a beautiful home and my family was happy. My wife, my children and my grandchildren have brought me so much happiness.

Epilogue

Now that I had survived the camps and started my life anew there were still two things that I wanted to do. First I wanted to find out what happened to Josef Ekhardt. The people in the Underground in Auschwitz had made a vow that if ever one of us could find Josef Ekhardt, we would do something about him. I also wanted to find out if the Count of Auschwitz had survived. If possible, I wanted to thank him for what he did, to let him know that some of us survived. For years, these things stayed on my mind.

In Toronto, I had joined a synagogue. I'm not Orthodox, but I wanted my children to have bar mitzvahs and Jewish weddings and Jewish spouses and so on. I am a Jew and I wanted Judaism to have some kind of a role in my life. Believing in it is another thing. After Auschwitz, it is not easy to believe. I had quite a few sessions with the rabbi about Judaism, about religion, about the Holocaust and lots of other things. We took a liking to each other.

Sometime in 1988, the rabbi called me to ask if I had seen the notice in the Jewish paper that the American Jewish Congress was looking for people who knew about guards from Auschwitz. They needed witnesses who could testify against some SS who were living in the United States. I got the paper and found in the article a list of twelve or fifteen names of German people who had immigrated to America and were suspected of being members of the SS. They all said that they had been in the military, not the SS, and the American Jewish Congress wanted to find out the truth. On that list I saw the name Josef Eckert. I was sure it was the man I remembered as commander of the ditches in Auschwitz. I called the rabbi back and told him that I would tell the American Jewish Congress what I knew. If they wanted me to be a witness, I would be a witness.

The rabbi called the Congress in Washington and talked to the man in charge. An hour later I got a call from a young man and we spoke for an hour. I told him that the Josef Ekhardt I knew was not an ordinary military guard, as he was claiming. I told him what he really was. A few days later he called me back and said that they had interrogated Eckert and he was still claiming that he had only been a guard in Auschwitz.

I was equally sure that it was the same man and suggested that the investigator find out if the man spoke Hungarian, because I knew that Josef Ekhardt was of Hungarian descent. There couldn't be two Josef Ekhardts in Auschwitz who both spoke Hungarian. I also suggested that they check under his arm to see if he had a tattoo with his blood type. The SS had their blood type tattooed in their armpit in case they were wounded and needed a blood transfusion – they could only receive "Aryan" blood, not Polish blood and certainly not Jewish blood. From what I knew, it had to be pure German blood, hopefully from someone in the Nazi Party. The American investigator told me that they had already checked and had found the mark on him.

Three days later the fellow in Washington phoned me again and told me excitedly that Eckert did speak Hungarian. They were planning to try him in the US but needed more documentation. His department was sending him to Austria to look for more evidence and if there was a trial, I would be the main witness.

Soon after our conversation he flew to Vienna and was able to accumulate quite a bit of information about Josef Eckert. He got in touch to report that he had the papers and was coming back. He flew to London and bought a ticket for Pan Am flight 103. That was the airplane that exploded in Lockerbie, Scotland, sabotaged by Libyans. The American investigator was killed and all the documentation was lost.

Throughout this whole process, neither of us realized that we were actually talking about two different men with similar names, spelled differently, that served in Auschwitz. One was Josef Eckert, a native of Yugoslavia, who was a low-ranking SS officer and the other was Josef Ekhardt, the man who I knew about because of his brutal behaviour as commander of the ditches in Auschwitz. The man they had arrested and subsequently deported was Josef Eckert. As far as I know, Josef Ekhardt might still be alive. In my dreams I meet up with the Count of Auschwitz and he takes on the case of prosecuting Ekhardt. In my mind, the Count of Auschwitz could catch that monster, which does justice to my memory of the Count as a man who played such a big part in my survival.

When I came out of Auschwitz alive, I told myself that one day I wanted to find the Count of Auschwitz to thank him for what he did. I hoped that he was still alive. He wasn't easy to find because I only knew his code name, but I figured I could start in Toronto with the British diplomats. I went to the British consulate and asked someone how I might find a POW who had been in Auschwitz. They said they would look into it for me because, after all, there hadn't been too many British POWs in Auschwitz.

I never heard from them. I waited and then I called again and went back to ask in person. They couldn't find anything. I kept pestering them. After about a year of trying to get to the bottom of it, they still couldn't find anything. They got tired of me calling and going there and finally gave me a telephone number in London, England. Phoning to London wasn't cheap, though. In a year I spent several hundred dollars. They called me back a few times, but there was no way they could find anything for me.

More years went by and one day I found a book about a man who saved a lot of lives during the war. There was a picture of a man in a British uniform on the cover. I took this book home and read it, but I didn't recognize anything about him. I was reading about the Count of Auschwitz and didn't realize it because I didn't know his real name. To me it was just an interesting story about a man who was at Dunkirk and was a POW. Then I got to the last chapter and it called him the "Count of Auschwitz." I thought I was going to faint as soon as I saw that. It turns out that his real name was Charles Coward. I was so happy to know his name that I didn't even finish the book.

I called the British consulate in Toronto again and I asked them how to find out about an ex-soldier. I gave them his name and told them the story. They suggested that I come to the consulate and write out what I was looking for; they would see what they could do. I did all of that, gave them my phone number and address and went home hoping that, at last, I would finally hear something. The staff at the consulate contacted the military headquarters in London. I waited. No answer. Time passed. A month passed, then two months. Three months later, I called the people I had spoken to in England. Again, their answer was, "We don't know anything about it." It seemed impossible to me that there could be a book written about him and yet the British government didn't know anything. I got really frustrated. By this time they already recognized my voice at the British consulate in Toronto, so I even went to the embassy in Ottawa. Nobody knew anything.

In a last-ditch attempt to find the Count, I asked the British staff to help me find the person who wrote the book and they gave me the name and contact information for the publisher. When I called them in London, however, although they were very nice, they didn't want to tell me anything either. Unfortunately, the author of the book was dead. No one seemed to be able to put me in touch with Charles Coward or his family. Another "sorry." Another "I don't know." I wondered why no one would give me any information. I sent a telegram. I phoned again. Finally the main editor at the publisher felt sorry for me when I told her that I couldn't afford to keep calling long distance from Toronto.

She told me that she wasn't supposed to give out the information, but she would tell Charles Coward's family who I was, what I wanted and give them my name and phone number. If they wanted to do something about it, it was up to them. I figured that this was another dead end but she did give my name to the family. Charles Coward's eldest son had immigrated to British Columbia and then moved to Ontario. He had been living nearby all the time that I was looking for his father. The family called him and told him my story.

When the son called me and told me who he was, I immediately jumped in the car and went to see him. It was a very emotional meeting. We kissed and hugged. We cried. He told me that he was sorry to tell me that his father had died about ten years before and would have given a lot to know that I had survived.

I finally found out why no one would give me any information: after Charles Coward had been a witness at the Nuremberg Trials in 1947 and had been honoured by Yad Vashem as a Righteous Gentile in 1965, he was in the news a lot. His son told me that neo-Nazis had targeted him, calling him a "Jew-lover" and burning his house. His family had had to move because of the threats and they were living in fear. Scotland Yard and the military police had promised to keep his whereabouts secret and when I came around asking questions, they had no idea who I was. I could have been one of the people out to get him. So by the time I found anything out, the Count was already dead. I never got to thank him in person.

I continued to see Coward's son once or twice a year. He gave me a picture of his father in his military uniform and told me many stories. When his mother got very sick and he couldn't afford to go to London, I bought him a ticket. Unfortunately, he died of a heart attack, leaving a wife and kids. I think that some of Charles Coward's other children are still alive, as well as grandchildren.

The other person I'd like to mention is Primo, the young Italian engineer in Buna. When he had said to me, "I am not ready to go to the gas chamber or to the Mosquito *Kommando*," I didn't know what he meant by the Mosquito *Kommando*," but I have since learned about it. I haven't seen it mentioned in any writing about Auschwitz. After the war, in Toronto, I met a German Jewish woman who had been in Auschwitz very early on in the war and had become first Dr. Mengele's assistant and then an assistant to Bruno Kitt, a German doctor in charge of the Mosquito *Kommando*. She told me the story of the Mosquito *Kommando* just six months before she died. It was in Block 10, a block she called the SS Lazarus, the domain of doctors who did horrific experiments on inmates. During the war, the Germans were fighting in Africa and soldiers were often bitten by mosquitoes that carried malaria, so they needed special medication. Nazi scientists were trying to develop something new but they needed human beings to test their formulas on so they took young, healthy Jewish men and women and used them for their experiments. When someone went into Block 10, they hardly ever came out alive.

This Mosquito *Kommando* was so secret that hardly anybody knew about it, nor was there any documentation. Primo must have overheard something about it in Buna where there were a lot of high-ranking SS officers overseeing the work at I. G. Farben. That's why when he refused to co-operate with the Underground, he said to me, "I am not ready for the gas chamber or for the Mosquito *Kommando*." It was one of the ultimate penalties.

And what happened to my friend Jakob? While we were working at the club in Gmunden, Jakob fell in love with an Austrian woman. He lied, at first saying that she was Jewish. I didn't want him to marry an Austrian girl and because of this we parted ways. They went to Paris and I came to Canada and we didn't see each other for a long time. I didn't talk to him for twenty years. Later on, we met up in Montreal, but it was never the same.

Jakob and his wife retired to Florida, where he belonged to an association of Holocaust survivors. Jakob told them about me and they asked me to participate in a video about Holocaust survivors. That was in January 1995, exactly fifty years after the liberation of Auschwitz. Jakob was putting together a party for the whole group one evening and must have thought there weren't enough drinks. He drove to the store and on the way back he was killed in a car accident. Instead of a party, we had a funeral for the man who had saved my life several times.

Jakob's daughter converted to Judaism. Jakob had told her about me and later she looked me up. We talked about Jakob and there was an instant connection between us.

I have four of my own kids, thank God. To be honest with you, I really didn't think that I could have any children, not after what I went through. When I married Regina, we thought that if I couldn't have any children, at least we loved each other. When she got pregnant, I felt like going to the top of the biggest mountain in the world and yelling, "I'm going to have a kid!" I don't think I can describe my happiness when my daughter Esther was born in Gmunden. A doctor came to the house and a midwife was there, too. I saw my daughter being born and I passed out flat on the floor. I always fainted so easily.

I have another daughter, Miriam, who was born in 1952. Then I have a son, Nathan, born in 1956 and another son, Ami, who was born in 1965. I named him Ami because in Hebrew it means "my people." And I have my grandchildren and now also my great-grandchildren. Esther's children are Toby and Naomi. Toby now has two children, Jackson and Presley and Naomi has a daughter named Chloë. Miriam's daughter, Leora, married recently. Nathan has two daughters, Fern and Brooke.

I'm still not religious. For me, the most important thing is my Zionist upbringing and my Zionist beliefs, belief in Israel and my deep connection to the Jewish faith. I still belong to a synagogue and I go there for bar mitzvahs and holidays.

The very first Yom Kippur after we were liberated, I fasted with Jakob and our other friends. I've never eaten on Yom Kippur since then because this is the day that I keep for the memory of the murder of my parents and brother. My kids honour this too. They don't eat on Yom Kippur in the memory of their grandparents.

I've been back to Poland. I looked for my parents again and I couldn't find records of what had happened to them. I learned that my father was somewhere in the Poznań area. Remember I mentioned that my father didn't come to the jail to say goodbye to me? That day, only my mother and my brother came to see me and they said they didn't know where he was. I found out from my aunt in Portugal that my father was also sent to a labour camp in the Poznań area. While there, he went to the commander at Poznań and asked for permission to send a letter to his sister in Portugal. The commander must have been humane because he let him write to her. You cannot say that all the Germans were monsters. He sent her a few letters and he was even allowed to send a photograph from the camp. I visited my aunt in Portugal and she gave me all of these to keep. She was the only one that survived. I never learned what happened to my parents or Romek, but from what I now know about what happened in the Lodz ghetto, I know it was impossible for my mother and my brother to survive.

There is a monument in Birkenau. Behind it, it's still Auschwitz. Whenever I go to Poland, I put flowers on the monument and say a prayer.

How did I survive? There is nothing more powerful than hate. I built such hatred inside me that it kept me going. Then little by little, that hate started disappearing because I had to build a new life. I was trying to become a human being again. Believe me, it wasn't easy. It was almost the same thing as when I stopped believing in God. I've seen what happened to my people, so how can I believe in God? There's supposed to be a God and apparently we are the Chosen People. We were chosen to go to the gas chambers and crematoria, so I stopped believing in God.

In my talks with the rabbi I said to him, "Rabbi, help me. What should I do? I don't believe in your God but I want my kids to believe in your God. My wife believes; her parents believe."

He didn't try to convince me. He was a smart guy. He didn't say,

"You have to." He said, "You don't have to believe. Just join the synagogue and don't worry about the rest of it." That's why I joined the
synagogue.

I know that I owe something to the people who didn't survive.
Maybe I was spared in order to tell their story, in hope that the world
won't forget them. I saw them die only because they were Jews. I hope
something like this never happens again – everyone should hope the
same. Unfortunately, genocides keep happening, in Cambodia, in
Africa, in Yugoslavia. Why?

When the kids were little, they asked me, "Daddy, what is this
number on your arm?" I joked with them that it was a telephone number for my girlfriend. I had to say something. Should I have taught
them hate? They cannot live in hate. To my grandchildren, I say, "Be
proud to be Jewish, live your life in full and be kind to others."

For me, it's something else. I bury my hate and try to live a normal
life. But I don't sleep well. As soon as I close my eyes, I'm in the camp.
I have nightmares, like the scene of bodies lying all over the field by
the ditches. But when I wake up, I know I'm Felix Opatowski, not
1 – 4 – 3 – 4 – 2 –5.

"The Song of the Partisans:" Zog Nit Keyn mol / Never Say

(Lyrics: Hersh Glick · Translation Reene Zufi)

Zog nit keyn mol as du geyst dem letsen veg
Chotsh himlen bleyene farshtelen bloye teg
Kimen vet doch undzer oysgebenkte sho
S'vet a poyk ton undzer trot mir zainen doh!

Fun grinem palmen land biz vayten land fun shnay
Mir kumen on mit undzer payn mit undzer vay
Un vu gefallen s'iz a shprits fun undzer blut
Shprotsn vet dort undzer gvure undzer mut

S'vet di morgn zun bagildn undz dem haynt
Un der nechtn vert geshvindn mit faynt
Nor oyb farzamen vet di zun un der kayor
Vi a parol zol gayn dos lid fun dor tsu dor

Dos lied geshribn iz mit blut un nit mit blay
S'iz nit kayn leidl fun a foygl oyf fray
Dos hot a folk tsvishen falndike vent
Does lied gezungen mit naganes in di hent.

To zog nit keyn mol az du geyst dem letstn veg,
Khotsh kimlen blayene farshteln bloye teg,
Kumen vet nokh undzer oysgebenkte sho -
S'vet a poyk ton undzer trot mir zainen doh!

Never say you are going on your final road,
Although leadened skies block out blue days,
Our longed-for hour will yet come
Our step will beat out – we are here!

From a land of green palm trees to the white land of snow
We arrive with our pain, with our woe,
Wherever a spurt of our blood fell,
On that spot shall spurt forth our courage and our spirit.

The morning sun will brighten our day
And yesterday will disappear with our foe.
But if the sun delays to rise at dawn,
Then let this song be a password for generations to come.

This song is written with our blood, not with lead,
It is not a song of a free bird flying overhead.
Amid crumbling walls, a people sang this song,
With grenades in their hands.

So, never say the road now ends for you,
Although skies of lead block out days of blue.
Our longed-for hour will yet come –
Our step will beat out – we are here!

Glossary

antisemitism Prejudice, discrimination, persecution and/or hatred against Jewish people, institutions, culture and symbols.

Appellplatz (German; the place for roll call) The area in Nazi camps where inmates had to assemble to be counted. Roll calls were part of a series of daily humiliations for prisoners, who were often made to stand completely still for hours, regardless of the temperature.

Auschwitz (German; in Polish, Oświęcim) A town in southern Poland approximately forty kilometres from Krakow, it is also the name of the largest complex of Nazi concentration camps that were built nearby. The Auschwitz complex contained three main camps: Auschwitz I, a slave labour camp built in May 1940; Auschwitz II-Birkenau, the death camp built in early 1942 where Felix Opatowski was interned from 1943 to 1945; and Auschwitz-Monowitz, a slave labour camp built in October 1942. In 1941 Auschwitz I was a testing site for usage of the lethal gas Zyklon B as a method of mass killing, which then went into wide usage. The Auschwitz complex was liberated by the Soviet army in January 1945.

bar mitzvah (Hebrew; literally, one to whom commandments apply) The age of thirteen when, according to Jewish tradition, boys become religiously and morally responsible for their actions and are considered adults for the purpose of synagogue ritual. A bar mitzvah is also the synagogue ceremony and family celebration that mark the attainment of this status, during which the boy is called upon to read a portion of the Torah and recite the pre-scribed prayers in a public prayer forum. In the latter half of the twentieth century, liberal Jews instituted an equivalent ceremony and celebration for girls – called a bat mitzvah.

Betar A Zionist youth movement founded by Revisionist Zion-ist leader Ze'ev Jabotinsky in 1923 that encouraged the develop-ment of a new generation of Zionist activists based on the ideals of courage, self-respect, military training, defence of Jewish life and property, and settlement in Israel to establish a Jewish state in British Mandate Palestine. In 1934, Betar membership in Po-land numbered more than 40,000. During the 1930s and 1940s, as antisemitism increased and the Nazis launched their murderous campaign against the Jews of Europe, Betar rescued thousands of Jews by organizing illegal immigration to British Mandate Pal-estine. The Betar movement today, closely aligned with Israel's right-wing Likud party, remains involved in supporting Jewish and Zionist activism around the world. *See also* Jabotinsky, Ze'ev.

Bindermichl DP camp A displaced persons camp located in Linz, Austria that housed approximately 2,500 people from October 1945 to March 1949. The Bindermichl camp was a social and cul-tural community for displaced Jews of post-war Europe. There were educational facilities and religious organizations, and news-papers produced by the residents were distributed to other DP camps in Austria. The Jewish Historical Commission was estab-lished there to document war crimes; it later became Simon Wi-esenthal's Jewish Historical Documentation Center.

Birkenau Also known as Auschwitz II. One of the camps that was part of the Auschwitz complex and operated as a death camp, the sole purpose of which was killing Jews and other people consid-ered undesirable by the Nazis. Established in early 1942, the gas chambers at Birkenau used Zyklon B gas for mass murder. The camp also held four crematoria that were constructed between March and June 1943. *See also* Auschwitz.

Blockstube (German) Office block.

Bricha (Hebrew; literally, escape) Name given to the massive organized, clandestine migration of Jews from Eastern Europe and DP camps to pre-state Israel following World War II. Estimates of the number of Jews helped by Bricha range from 80,000 to 250,000. Although the goal of the organization was to smuggle Jews out to pre-state Israel, Felix Opatowski, among others, used the group and its connections to escape from Poland into DP camps in Austria and Germany.

British Mandate Palestine The area under British rule established by the League of Nations after World War I. Currently encompassing present-day Israel, Jordan, the West Bank and the Gaza Strip, the land was administrated by the United Kingdom – which restricted Jewish immigration – between 1923 and 1948.

Buna Also called Buna-Monowitz or Auschwitz III, Buna was a subcamp of Auschwitz that housed more than 10,000 slave labourers who worked in the nearby I. G. Farben industry works. It was built in October 1942 in the formerly Polish village of Monowice (in German, Monowitz). *See also* I. G. Farben; Monowitz.

cheder (Hebrew; literally, room) An Orthodox Jewish elementary school that teaches the fundamentals of Jewish religious observance and textual study, as well as the Hebrew language.

Coward, Charles (1905–1976) A British prisoner of war (POW) who was held in the E715 camp that existed at Auschwitz between September 1943 and January 1945. The British prisoners at the camp, which was several metres west of the I. G. Farben construction site and near the Buna-Monowitz subcamp, were forced to work at the Farben site. Charles Coward, who had previously escaped from numerous POW camps, was sent to camp E715 in December 1943. As the camp's Red Cross liaison, he had a certain amount

of freedom to move around the subcamp and into the surrounding towns. Known officially as the "British Man of Confidence"
because he both represented his fellow soldiers' interests and
was in communication with the Germans in charge of the POW
camp, his role led to the coining of his nickname, the "Count of
Auschwitz." After the war, Coward testified at the Nuremberg Trials about the gas chambers at Birkenau and the dehumanizing
conditions he witnessed at Auschwitz. There has also been much
documentation about Coward's success in smuggling messages
out to the British government about Auschwitz and about British POWs helping Jewish inmates by smuggling food and other
items to them. In the 1954 book about his exploits during the war,
The Password Is Courage, there is a lengthy description of Coward
smuggling ammunition into Auschwitz-Birkenau, although these
claims have never been substantiated. The 1962 movie of the same
name, based on the book, focused more on Coward's escapes
from other POW camps prior to his arrival near Buna-Monowitz.
Coward was awarded the title of Righteous Among the Nations
by Yad Vashem in 1965 and posthumously, in 2010, the British
government named him a British Hero of the Holocaust. *See also*
Buna; Nuremberg Trials; Righteous Among the Nations.

Cyrankiewicz, Józef (1911–1989) Prime minister of the People's Republic of Poland from 1947–1952 and 1954–1970, Józef Cyrankiewicz also served as head of state between 1970 and 1972. A socialist who was active in the resistance movement of the Polish
Home Army at the start of World War II in 1939, he was arrested
by German armed forces in 1941 and imprisoned until September
1942, when he was transferred to Auschwitz. During his incarceration in the camp, he joined the underground Polish resistance
group and helped get messages to the outside world. He was sent
on the death march to Mauthausen in January 1945 and eventually liberated there by US troops. *See also* Polish Underground in
Auschwitz.

Czech Family Camp (Auschwitz) A section of the Birkenau "quarantine" camp, where recent arrivals were housed temporarily, that was reserved for the more than 10,000 Czech Jewish prisoners who were deported from the Theresienstadt camp between September and December 1943. For approximately six months, the Czech Jews were accorded privileges such as receiving parcels and writing letters in an effort to counteract rumours that the Nazis were annihilating Jews, but they were eventually subjected to the same fate as other prisoners at Birkenau. Thousands were murdered in the gas chambers on March 8 and 9, 1944; a few months later, in July, after a selection that found only a few thousand fit for forced labour, the rest of the family camp, more than seven thousand Czech Jews, were sent to the gas chambers. *See also* Theresienstadt.

Dachau The Nazis' first concentration camp, established to house primarily political prisoners in March 1933. The Dachau camp was located about sixteen kilometres northwest of Munich in southern Germany. The number of Jews interned there rose considerably after the Kristallnacht pogroms on the night of November 9–10, 1938. In 1942 a crematorium area was constructed next to the main camp. By the spring of 1945, Dachau and its subcamps held more than 67,665 registered prisoners – 43,350 categorized as political prisoners and 22,100 as Jews. As the American Allied forces neared the camp in April 1945, the Nazis forced 7,000 prisoners, primarily Jews, on a gruelling death march to the Tegernsee camp in southern Germany. *See also* Kristallnacht.

displaced persons (DPs) People who find themselves homeless and stateless at the end of a war. Following World War II, millions of people, especially European Jews, found that they had no homes to return to or that it was unsafe to do so. To resolve the staggering refugee crisis that resulted, Allied authorities and the United Nations Relief and Rehabilitation Administration (UNRRA) established Displaced Persons (DP) camps to provide temporary shelter and assistance to refugees, and help them transition towards resettlement. *See also* DP camps.

DP camps Facilities set up by the Allied authorities and the United Nations Relief and Rehabilitation Administration (UNRRA) in October 1945 to resolve the refugee crisis that arose at the end of World War II. The camps provided temporary shelter and assistance to the millions of people – not only Jews – who had been displaced from their home countries as a result of the war and helped them prepare for resettlement.

Ebensee A town in upper Austria located seventy-five kilometres southwest of Linz that was also the site of a forced labour camp, a subcamp of the Mauthausen complex, from November 1943 until May 1945. Forced labourers at Ebensee were used to build tunnels to conceal ammunition. The conditions in the camp were deplorable and more than 20,000 prisoners died there. *See also* Mauthausen.

Eichmann, Adolf (1906–1962) Head of the Gestapo department responsible for the implementation of the Nazis' policy of mass murder of Jews (the so-called Final Solution). Eichmann's plan included industrialized mass killing facilities and mobile killing units to eradicate the Jewish populations of Eastern Europe and the USSR. He was captured in Argentina in 1960 by Israeli intelligence operatives and his ensuing 1961 trial in Israel was widely and internationally televised. Eichmann was sentenced to death and hanged in May 1962. *See also* Gestapo.

Gestapo (German) Short for Geheime Staatspolizei, the Secret State Police of Nazi Germany. The Gestapo was the brutal force that dealt with the perceived enemies of the Nazi regime and were responsible for rounding up European Jews for deportation to the death camps. They operated with very few legal constraints and were also responsible for issuing exit visas to the residents of German-occupied areas. In the camp system, Gestapo officials ran the Politische Abteilung (Political Department), which was responsible for prisoner registration, surveillance, investigation and interrogation.

ghetto A confined residential area for Jews. The term originated in Venice, Italy in 1516 with a law requiring all Jews to live on a segregated, gated island known as Ghetto Nuovo. Throughout the Middle Ages in Europe, Jews were often forcibly confined to gated Jewish neighbourhoods. During the Holocaust, the Nazis forced Jews to live in crowded and unsanitary conditions in rundown districts of cities and towns. Most ghettos in Poland were enclosed by brick walls or wooden fences with barbed wire. *See also* Lodz ghetto.

Gymnasium (German) A word used throughout central and eastern Europe to mean high school.

Gypsy The term for the Sinti and Roma people commonly used in the past, and now generally considered to be derogatory. The Sinti and Roma are a nomadic people who speak Romani, an Indo-European language. During the Holocaust, which the Roma refer to in Romani as the *Porajmos* – the devouring – they were stripped of their citizenship under the Nuremberg Laws and were targeted for death under Hitler's race policies. In Auschwitz-Birkenau, more than 20,000 Sinti and Roma were segregated into the "Gypsy camp" and then systematically murdered. The estimation of how many Roma were killed during World War II varies widely and has been difficult to document – estimations generally range from between 200,000 to 1,000,000. *See also* Nuremberg Laws.

Heydrich, Reinhard (1904–1942) Chief of the Reich Main Security Office (overseeing both the SD, the Nazi intelligence service, and the Gestapo) and one of the orchestrators of the "Final Solution" – the Nazi plan for the systematic murder of Europe's Jewish population. Heydrich's brutality toward Czech citizens earned him the nickname the "Butcher of Prague." In May 1942, Heydrich was attacked in Prague by British soldiers on behalf of the Czechoslovak government-in-exile and succumbed to his injuries from the assassination attempt one week later.

high holidays (also High Holy Days) The autumn holidays that mark the beginning of the Jewish year and that include Rosh Hashanah (New Year) and Yom Kippur (Day of Atonement). Rosh Hashanah is observed by synagogue services where the leader of the service blows the shofar (ram's horn), and festive meals where sweet foods, such as apples and honey, are eaten to symbolize and celebrate a sweet new year. Yom Kippur, a day of fasting and prayer at synagogue, follows ten days later.

Höss, Rudolf (1900–1947) The first commandant of Auschwitz and chief planner of the camp's use as a facility for mass murder. After the war, Höss was tried for murder by the Polish Supreme National Tribunal in Warsaw and hanged in 1947 at the gallows in Auschwitz.

I. G. Farben A German chemical corporation that collaborated with the Nazis during World War II and held the patent for the Zyklon B gas crystals that were used in the Auschwitz gas chambers. One of their five plants was a synthetic rubber and oil factory in Buna-Monowitz (also known Auschwitz III) that used thousands of slave labourers from Auschwitz. After the war, the I. G. Farben war crimes trial, part of the Nuremberg Trials, resulted in twenty-four directors being tried for war crimes; of those, thirteen were found guilty and sentenced to prison terms ranging from one to eight years. *See also* Auschwitz; Nuremberg Trials.

International Refugee Organization An organization established in 1948 by the United Nations to deal with the refugee crisis emanating from World War II. It was the successor agency to the United Nations Relief and Rehabilitation Administration (UNRRA) and precursor to the Office of the High Commissioner for Refugees established in 1952 (now the United Nations High Commissioner for Refugees). *See also* displaced persons; United Nations Relief and Rehabilitation Administration (UNRRA).

Jabotinsky, Ze'ev (1880–1940) The founder of the Revisionist Zionist movement who established his own branch of nationalist Zionism, the New Zionist Organization, in 1935. Jabotinsky strongly urged European Jews to immigrate to British Mandate Palestine and met with the governments of Hungary, Poland and Romania to advocate this "evacuation plan." He believed in establishing a Jewish state in Palestine with the support of Jewish brigades and his movement strongly advocated Jewish self-defence and self-determination. Ze'ev Jabotinsky was also commander of the Irgun, the underground Jewish military organization that operated in Palestine between 1937 and 1948. *See also* Betar.

Jewish Committee (post-war) Also called the Central Committee of Polish Jews (in Polish: Centralny Komitet Zydow Polsce, or CKZP). An organization established in 1944 and officially recognized as the highest administrative body of Polish Jewry, the Central Committee sought to reconstruct post-war Jewish life in Poland. The CKZP set up various departments to help survivors search for their families and document their testimonies. The organization also provided legal assistance, social services and health care, established orphanages, and disseminated reports and newsletters on the state of Jewish life in post-war Poland.

Jewish ghetto police (in German, Ordnungsdienst; literally, Order Service) The Jewish ghetto police force established by the Jewish Councils (*Judenräte*) on the orders of the Germans. They were armed with clubs and carried out the orders of the Germans. There has been much debate and controversy surrounding the role of the Jewish Councils and the Jewish police. *See also* Judenrat.

Judenrat (German; pl. *Judenräte*) Jewish Council. A group of Jewish leaders appointed by the Germans to administer and provide services to the local Jewish population under occupation and carry out German orders. The *Judenräte* appeared to be self-governing entities, but were under complete German control. The *Judenräte* faced difficult and complex moral decisions under brutal conditions and remain a contentious subject. The chairmen had to

decide whether to comply or refuse to comply with German demands. Some were killed by the Nazis for refusing, while others
committed suicide. Jewish officials who advocated compliance
thought that cooperation might save at least some Jews. Some
who denounced resistance efforts did so because they believed
that armed resistance would bring death to the entire community.

K-ration Non-perishable, individually packaged food rations distributed by the US Army to soldiers during World War II.

Kamerad (German; pl. *Kameraden*) Comrade.

Kanada *Kommando* A prisoner work detail in Auschwitz given the
task of sorting through the belongings and clothing confiscated
from newly arrived prisoners. The name, adopted by the prisoners working there, came from the widely held belief that Canada was a land of wealth, thus its association with the enormous
amount of goods seized by the camp authorities. The warehouses
that stored the goods were also referred to as Kanada.

kapo (German) A concentration camp prisoner appointed by the SS
to oversee other prisoners working as slave labourers.

Kommando (German; literally, unit or command) Forced work details that were set up by the Nazi labour and concentration camp
administrators during World War II.

Kristallnacht (German; literally, Night of Broken Glass) A series of
pogroms that took place in Germany and Austria on November
9–10, 1938. Over the course of twenty-four hours, ninety-one Jews
were murdered, 25,000–30,000 were arrested and deported to
concentration camps, two hundred synagogues were destroyed
and thousands of Jewish businesses and homes were ransacked.
Planned by the Nazis as a coordinated attack on the Jews of Germany and Austria, Kristallnacht is often seen as an important
turning point in Hitler's policies of systematic persecution of
Jews. *See also* pogrom.

L'chaim (Hebrew; to life) A toast recited at celebrations such as weddings and bar/bat mitzvahs.

Levi, Primo (1919–1987) Italian Jewish chemist and writer who was incarcerated in Auschwitz III, working for the I. G. Farben company, from February 1944 to January 1945. Levi published many essays and works of poetry and is best known for his Auschwitz memoir *If This Is A Man* (1947; re-published in 1958).

Lodz ghetto A restricted area for Jews in the Baluty district of the Polish city of Lodz. It was the second-largest ghetto in German-occupied Eastern Europe, after the Warsaw Ghetto. The ghetto was sealed off on May 1, 1940, with a population of more than 160,000 Jews. Initially intended as a temporary holding place for the Jews of Lodz until they could be deported, its organizational structure served as a model for the establishment of other ghettos. Most of the ghetto inhabitants worked as slave labourers in factories, primarily in the textile industry. The dissolution of the Lodz Ghetto began in the summer of 1944 with the deportation of most of its inhabitants to the Chelmno death camp or Auschwitz. The few who remained were liberated by the Soviet Red Army in January 1945. The Lodz Ghetto outlasted all the other ghettos established by the Nazis in Eastern Europe.

Magazine (German) Warehouse.

Mauthausen A notoriously brutal Nazi concentration camp located about twenty kilometres east of the Austrian city of Linz. First established in 1936 shortly after the annexation of Austria to imprison "asocial" political opponents of the Third Reich, the camp grew to encompass fifty nearby subcamps and became the largest forced labour complex in the German-occupied territories. By the end of the war, close to 200,000 prisoners had passed through the Mauthausen forced labour camp system and almost 120,000 of them died there – including 38,120 Jews – from starvation, disease and hard labour. Mauthausen was classified as a Category 3 camp, which indicated the harshest conditions, and inmates were often worked to death in the brutal Wiener-Graben stone quarry. The US army liberated the camp on May 5, 1945.

Mein Kampf (German; My Struggle) Adolf Hitler's manifesto for his National Socialist movement that appeared in two volumes in 1925 and 1926 (though the second volume was dated 1927). The book combines autobiography with a delineation of Hitler's racist, antisemitic, ultra-nationalist, anti-democratic and anti-Marxist ideology. It was widely disseminated across Germany following Hitler's rise to power in 1933. Today, the book is considered hate speech and selling or trading it is restricted in many countries.

Melk An Austrian town about one hundred kilometres east of the city of Linz that was also the site of one of the subcamps of the Mauthausen concentration camp complex. The Melk subcamp existed from April 1944 until April 1945 and functioned as a forced labour camp that used prisoners to build quartz tunnels in the surrounding mountains. More than 10,000 people died in Melk, which also had a gas chamber and a crematorium.

Mengele, Josef (1911–1979) The most notorious of about thirty SS garrison physicians in Auschwitz, Mengele was stationed at the camp from May 1943 to January 1945. From May 1943 to August 1944, Mengele was the medical officer of the Birkenau "Gypsy Camp"; from August 1944 until Auschwitz was evacuated in January 1945, Mengele became Chief Medical Officer of the main infirmary camp in Birkenau. One of the camp doctors responsible for deciding which prisoners were fit for slave labour and which were to be immediately sent to the gas chambers, he was also known for conducting sadistic experiments on Jewish and Roma prisoners, especially twins.

Mischling (German; pl. *Mischlinge*; literally, crossbreed) During World War II, *Mischling* was a term used to denote Germans who were of only partial Aryan ancestry and therefore subject to persecution under Hitler's racial policies enacted as the Nuremberg Laws. The edicts included a legal test to determine whether someone was a *Mischling* and, if so, the "degree" or category that defined his or her status. *See also* Nuremberg Laws.

Moll, Otto (1915–1946) A member of the SS who was transferred to Auschwitz to head up the mass grave-digging work detail in 1941. Moll became chief of the crematoria at Auschwitz-Birkenau in 1943 and was known for his volatility and particularly sadistic brutality toward prisoners. After the war, Moll was tried at the American Military Tribunal in Dachau, where he was sentenced to death.

Monowitz (German; in Polish, Monowice) Also known as Monowitz-Buna or Auschwitz III, Monowitz was originally a village in southern Poland approximately forty-five kilometres from Krakow. In October 1942 the village residents were evacuated in order to construct a forced labour camp for the nearby I. G. Farben Buna-Werke (Buna Works) industrial complex. Krupp, the German armaments manufacturer, also built a factory near Monowitz. *See also* Buna; I. G. Farben.

Muselmann (German; Muslim) A slang term used by camp prisoners to describe prisoners who were near death and seemed to have lost the will to live. Some scholars attribute the use of the word Muslim to the fact that the prostrate and dying prisoners were reminiscent of devout Muslims at prayer.

Nuremberg Laws The September 1935 laws that stripped Jews of their civil rights as German citizens and separated them from Germans legally, socially and politically. They were first announced at the Nazi party rally in the city of Nuremberg in 1933. Under "The Law for the Protection of German Blood and Honour" Jews were defined as a separate race rather than a religious group; whether a person was racially Jewish was determined by ancestry (how many Jewish grandparents a person had). Among other things, the law forbade marriages or sexual relations between Jews and Germans. *See also* Mischling.

Nuremberg Trials The war crimes trials that were held following Germany's surrender on May 7, 1945, in the German city of

Nuremberg. From November 21, 1945 to October 1, 1946, twenty-two of the major Nazi leaders and their collaborators stood trial for war crimes. Twelve subsequent trials, including the I. G. Farben trial, were held in front of military tribunals from December 9, 1946, to April 13, 1949.

Orthodox Judaism The set of beliefs and practices of Jews for whom the observance of Jewish law is closely connected to faith; it is characterized by strict religious observance of Jewish dietary laws, restrictions on work on the Sabbath and holidays, and a modest code of dress.

pogrom (Russian; to wreak havoc, to demolish) A violent attack on a distinct ethnic group. The term most commonly refers to 19th and 20th century attacks on Jews in the Russian Empire. *See also* Kristallnacht.

Polish Home Army (in Polish, Armia Krajowa) Also known as AK or the Home Army. Formed in February 1942, the Polish Home Army was the largest Polish resistance movement in German-occupied Poland during World War II. Although the organization has been criticized for antisemitism and some factions were even guilty of killing Jews, it is also true that the AK established a Section for Jewish Affairs that collected information about what was happening to Jews in Poland, centralized contacts between Polish and Jewish military organizations, and supported the Relief Council for Jews in Poland. Between 1942 and 1945, hundreds of Jews joined the AK. Members of the AK also assisted the Jewish revolt during the Warsaw Ghetto Uprising in 1943, both outside the ghetto walls and by joining Jewish fighters inside the ghetto. Although the Home Army was in touch with resistance groups in Auschwitz, they did not support the timing of the uprising there because they did not think they had enough resources for it to succeed.

Polish Underground in Auschwitz A resistance group established in Auschwitz as early as 1940 by Polish Home Army officer Witold

Pilecki. There were several Polish underground resistance groups in the camp that helped members cope with their circumstances by giving them news and extra food; their primary purpose was to send news of the camp's atrocities to the underground army in Warsaw. By late 1941, the disparate resistance groups had merged and Pilecki was planning a prisoners' revolt, but he did not have the cooperation of the Polish Home Army. After Pilecki escaped from Auschwitz in April 1943 to personally deliver information to leaders in Warsaw, the underground continued to organize under new command. Pilecki continued to work for the Home Army and fought to liberate Warsaw in 1944. He was captured and spent the rest of the war in a German POW camp.

Post Exchange (PX) Stores with subsidized goods set up by the US government for military personnel posted in foreign countries.

Red Cross The International Red Cross is a humanitarian organization founded in 1863 to protect the victims of war. During WWII the Red Cross provided assistance to prisoners of war by distributing food parcels and monitoring the situation in POW camps through their appointed liaisons. Today, in addition to the international body, there are National Red Cross and Red Crescent societies in almost every country in the world.

Reichstag The German parliament. When arsonists burned the building on February 27, 1933, Nazis accused Communists of setting the fire and many Communist members of parliament were arrested. The day after, the Decree of the Reich President for the Protection of People and State was passed (more commonly known as the Reichstag Fire Decree), which suspended the right to assembly, freedom of speech, freedom of the press and other constitutional protections, including all restraints on police investigations. The passage of the decree was an essential step in establishing the Third Reich as a one-party totalitarian state.

Righteous Among the Nations A title bestowed by Yad Vashem, the Holocaust Martyrs' and Heroes' Remembrance Authority in Jerusalem, to honour non-Jews who risked their lives to help save Jews during the Holocaust. A commission was established in 1963 to award the title. If a person fits certain criteria and the story is carefully corroborated, the honouree is awarded with a medal and certificate and commemorated on the Wall of Honour at the Garden of the Righteous in Jerusalem.

Rumkowski, Mordechai Chaim (1877–1944) The chief administrator of the Lodz ghetto appointed by the German authorities as head of the Jewish Council (or "Elder of the Jews"). He was in charge of all the Jewish public agencies and institutions in the ghetto, as well as the Jewish police. He also replaced German currency with special ghetto money, signed by himself, that came to be known as "Rumkies." Rumkowski was and remains a somewhat controversial figure because of his decisions to cooperate with the Germans in order to serve what he felt were the best interests of the Lodz ghetto inhabitants. Rumkowski served in this capacity from the time that the ghetto was established on February 8, 1940, until its dissolution in the summer of 1944, when he was deported to Auschwitz.

Schindler, Oskar (1908–1974) The German businessman who saved the lives of more than 1,000 Jews, who are often referred to as *Schindlerjuden* (Schindler's Jews). Schindler, a member of the Nazi party, took over an enamel factory situated close to the Płaszów labour camp in 1940 and began employing Jewish workers there, sheltering them from the harsh conditions at the camp. When his enamel factory, Emalia, was forced to close in 1944 as the Soviet troops advanced, he heroically rescued more than 1,000 Jews from deportation to Auschwitz by declaring them to be essential to the war effort and transporting them to his new ammunitions factory in Brünnlitz, Sudetenland. Oskar Schindler was awarded the title of Righteous Among the Nations by Yad Vashem in 1993 and was the subject of Steven Spielberg's 1993 film *Schindler's List*, based on the novel *Schindler's Ark* by Thomas Keneally.

Schreibstube (German) An administrative office.

scrip A form of replacement currency that operates like a credit system. Scrip was used by the American military in Germany and Austria instead of currency, and soldiers could exchange it in places of business that had links with the US government and participated in the system.

shtiebl (Yiddish; little house or little room) A small, unadorned prayer room or prayer house furnished like synagogues but much more modestly. Most observant Jews in Eastern Europe prayed in shtiebls on a daily basis; they attended services in a synagogue on holidays or sometimes on Shabbat, the weekly day of rest beginning Friday at sunset and ending Saturday at sundown.

Sonderkommando (German; special unit) Concentration camp prisoners charged with removing corpses from the gas chambers, loading them into the crematoria and disposing of the remains.

"Sonderkommando Uprising" A coordinated attempt by *Sonderkommando* workers to destroy the crematoria facilities at Auschwitz-Birkenau on October 7, 1944.

"The Song of the Partisans" A resistance song written by Jewish poet and partisan Hersh Glik while he was in the ghetto in Vilnius, Lithuania. The song, an emblem of hope and defiance, quickly spread to many prisoners in Nazi camps. It was eventually translated into Hebrew, Polish, Russian, Spanish, Romanian, Dutch and English.

Spanish Civil War (1936–1939) The war in Spain between the military – supported by Conservative, Catholic and fascist elements, together called the Nationalists – and the Republican government. Sparked by an initial coup that failed to win a decisive victory, the country was plunged into a bloody civil war. It ended when the Nationalists, under the leadership of General Francisco Franco, marched into Madrid. During the civil war, the Nationalists received aid from both Fascist Italy and Nazi Germany, and the Republicans received aid from volunteers worldwide.

spiel (German; in Yiddish, shpil) A persuasive speech or argument.

SS Abbreviation for Schutzstaffel (Defence Corps). The SS was established in 1925 as Adolf Hitler's elite corps of personal bodyguards. Under the direction of Heinrich Himmler, its membership grew from 280 in 1929 to 50,000 when the Nazis came to power in 1933, and to nearly a quarter of a million on the eve of World War II. The SS was comprised of the Allgemeine-SS (General SS) and the Waffen-SS (Armed, or Combat SS). The General SS dealt with policing and the enforcement of Nazi racial policies in Germany and the Nazi-occupied countries. An important unit within the SS was the Reichssicherheitshauptamt (RSHA, the Central Office of Reich Security), whose responsibility included the Gestapo (Geheime Staatspolizei). The SS ran the concentration and death camps, with all their associated economic enterprises, and also fielded its own Waffen-SS military divisions, including some recruited from the occupied countries. *See also* Gestapo.

SS *St. Louis* An ocean liner that sailed from Hamburg, Germany on May 13, 1939, with 937 passengers on board, most of them German Jewish refugees fleeing the Nazis. Their destination was Cuba, where they sought temporary refuge before being admitted into the United States. Both countries, however, refused entry to the passengers – as did Canada – and the ship was forced to return to Europe, eventually docking in Belgium. Passengers were given refuge in Britain, France, Belgium and Holland, but after the May 1940 Nazi invasion of France and the Low Countries, the passengers were once again targets of Nazi persecution. It is estimated that approximately 250 perished in the Holocaust.

Stalin, Joseph (1878–1953) The leader of the Soviet Union from 1924 until his death in 1953. Born Joseph Vissarionovich Dzhugashvili, he changed his name to Stalin (literally: man of steel) in 1903. He was a staunch supporter of Lenin, taking control of the Communist Party upon Lenin's death. Very soon after acquiring leadership of the Communist Party, Stalin ousted rivals, killed opponents in purges, and effectively established himself as a dictator. After World War II, Stalin set up Communist governments controlled by Moscow in many Eastern European states bordering and close to the USSR, and instituted antisemitic campaigns and purges.

Star of David (in Hebrew, *Magen David*) The six-pointed star that is the ancient and most recognizable symbol of Judaism. During World War II, Jews in Nazi-occupied areas were frequently forced to wear a badge or armband with the Star of David on it as an identifying mark of their lesser status and to single them out as targets for persecution.

Theresienstadt (German; in Czech, Terezin) A walled town in the Czech Republic, sixty kilometres north of Prague, that served as both a ghetto and a concentration camp between 1941 and 1945. More than 73,000 Jews from the German Protectorate of Bohemia and Moravia and from the Greater German Reich (including Austria and parts of Poland) were deported to Theresienstadt between November 24, 1941, and March 30, 1945, the majority of them arriving in 1942. More than 60,000 of them were deported from Theresienstadt to Auschwitz or other death camps. Theresienstadt was showcased as a "model" ghetto for propaganda purposes to demonstrate to delegates from the International Red Cross and others the "humane" treatment of Jews and to counter information reaching the Allies about Nazi atrocities and mass murder. The ghetto was liberated on May 8, 1945 by the Soviet Red Army.

United Nations Relief and Rehabilitation Administration (UNRRA) An organization created at a 44-nation conference in Washington, DC on November 9, 1943, to provide economic assistance to Nazi-occupied European nations following World War II and to repatriate and assist war refugees.

Volksdeutsche The term used by the Nazis to refer to the ethnic Germans living outside Germany in Central and Eastern Europe. Prior to World War II, there were more than 10 million ethnic

Germans living in these countries, some of whose families had been there for centuries. When the Nazis occupied these territories, they intended to reclaim the *Volksdeutsche* as Germans and strengthen their communities as a central part of creating the Nazis' ideal of a Greater Germany. Ethnic Germans were often given the choice to either sign the *Volksliste*, the list of German people, and be regarded as traitors by their home countries, or not to sign and be treated as traitors to the "Germanic race" by the Nazi occupiers. After the collapse of Nazi Germany most *Volksdeutsche* were persecuted by the post-war authorities in their home countries.

Wallenberg, Raoul (1912–1947) The Swedish diplomat who was sent to Hungary in June 1944 by the US Refugee Board and succeeded in saving tens of thousands of Budapest Jews by issuing them Swedish certificates of protection. The Swedish government also authorized Wallenberg to set up thirty "safe houses" and organize food distribution, medical assistance and child care for Jews in Budapest. Of the slightly more than 100,000 Jews that remained alive in Budapest at the end of the war (out of a pre-war population of 247,000), the majority were saved through his efforts. Wallenberg was awarded the title of Righteous Among the Nations by Yad Vashem in 1986 and has been honoured by memorials or monuments in ten other countries.

Warsaw Ghetto Uprising The largest single revolt by Jews during the Holocaust, the Warsaw Ghetto Uprising developed in response to the Nazis deportation of more than 275,000 ghetto inhabitants to slave-labour and death camps and the murder of another 10,000 of them between July and September 1942. When the Germans began planning to murder the ghetto's remaining population of approximately 60,000 Jews by deporting them to the Treblinka death camp on April 19, 1943, about 750 organized ghetto fighters launched an insurrection. Despite some support from Jewish and Polish resistance organizations outside the ghetto, the poorly armed insurgents were crushed by the Germans after a month on May 16, 1943. More than 56,000 Jews were captured; about 7,000 were shot and the remainder were deported to death camps and concentration camps.

Wiesel, Elie (1928) The Romanian-born Nobel Peace Prize Laureate, celebrated author, political activist and Holocaust survivor who was interned at Auschwitz from May 1944 until January 1945. Wiesel, who worked as a slave labourer in Buna-Monowitz and was later interned in Buchenwald, wrote about his experiences during the Holocaust in his book *Night*, a bestseller that has been translated into thirty languages. He has written more than fifty other books.

Yad Vashem The Holocaust Martyrs' and Heroes' Remembrance Authority established in 1953 to commemorate, educate the public about, research and document the Holocaust. *See also* Righteous Among the Nations.

Yiddish A language derived from Middle High German with elements of Hebrew, Aramaic, Romance and Slavic languages, and written in Hebrew characters. Spoken by Jews in east-central Europe for roughly a thousand years from the tenth century to the mid-twentieth century, it was still the most common language among European Jews until the outbreak of World War II. There are similarities between Yiddish and contemporary German.

Zionism A movement promoted by the Viennese Jewish journalist Theodor Herzl, who argued in his 1896 book *Der Judenstaat* (The Jewish State) that the best way to resolve the problem of antisemitism and persecution of Jews in Europe was to create an independent Jewish state in the historic Jewish homeland of Biblical Israel. Zionists also promoted the revival of Hebrew as a Jewish national language.

Photographs

1   Felix Opatowski's father, Nathan Opatowski, seated in the front row, far left, in the forced labour camp in Poznań stadium, circa 1940.

2   Felix and his friends in front of the American military club on the US army base in Gmunden, Austria, where they worked after the war. Felix is seated in the front row, far right, and his friend Jakob Artman is in the back row, centre, circa 1946.

1 A remnant of Felix's prison uniform from Birkenau showing his prisoner number.
2 Felix in front of the ruins of Barracks 24, where he was incarcerated in Birkenau. Felix, left, is beside Rudy Fidel, a pastor from Faith Temple in Winnipeg, and Rudy's wife, Gina, on a tour they took in 2009 to re-visit Felix's past.
3 The ruins of crematorium II, Birkenau, 2005.

1 Jakob Artman, Felix's friend who helped him survive in Auschwitz Birkenau, circa 1948.

2 Dr. Klaus, the Jewish doctor in the Melk concentration camp, who looked after Felix in the Melk hospital. The photo was taken in Gmunden, Austria, circa 1946.

3 Charles Coward, the "Count of Auschwitz," a British prisoner of war in Buna-Monowitz (Auschwitz III) who took part in resistance activities and tried to help Jews. He was later named a Righteous Among the Nations by Yad Vashem in Jerusalem. The photo was taken circa 1950.

4 Felix and his wife, Regina, at the tree planted in Charles Coward's honour in the Garden of the Righteous at Yad Vashem, Jerusalem, 2005.

Felix and Regina's wedding, June 16, 1947, Gmunden, Austria.

1 & 2 Felix's Certificate of Identity, which served as his travel visa to Canada in 1949, issued by the International Refugee Organization.

3 Felix and Regina in Gmunden, Austria, 1948.

4 Felix and Regina's daughter Esther, age 3, 1950.

1 Felix and Regina with their daughters. Miriam (left), about one year, and Esther (right), six years old. Toronto, circa 1953.

2 Felix and Regina's son Ami in Toronto, 1981.

3 The Opatowski family in 1964 on a cruise in Miami Beach, Florida. Regina and Esther are in the back row, and in the front (left to right), are Nathan, Miriam and Felix.

4 The house that Felix built in 1967 at 48 Purdon Dr., Toronto, where the Opatowskis lived for twenty-five years.

1   Esther and Miriam with their grandparents, Hillel and Bronia Gnat, at their uncle's wedding at Adath Israel in Toronto in 1966. Left to right: Esther, a relative, Hillel Gnat, Bronia Gnat and Miriam.

2   Regina's mother, Bronia Gnat, (left), Regina (centre), and Felix's aunt from Portugal, Sarah Krull (née Opatowski), circa 1970.

3   Felix and Regina on their 25th wedding anniversary, 1972. The photo was taken by their daughter Miriam.

1 Felix at the Birkenau monument, 2003.
2 Felix, third from the left, at the gates of Auschwitz on a 2005 trip organized by Beth Emeth synagogue for the 60th anniversary of the liberation of the camp.
3 Felix and Regina with their granddaughters Leora (left) and Naomi (right) in Auschwitz, 2005.
4 Felix with Gina Fidel in Birkenau in 2009, standing in an area of the Neutral Zone, where Felix worked when he was an inmate.

1 Felix and his great-granddaughter Chloë in 2011.

2 Felix and Regina with their great-grandchildren Chloë and Presley.

3 Women from the Opatowski family in Toronto in 2011. Left to right (back): Esther; Esther's daughter, Naomi; Miriam. Left to right (front): Toby's wife, Jodi; Toby's daughter, Presley; Regina; Naomi's daughter, Chloë; and Miriam's daughter, Leora.

4 Men from the Opatowski family in Toronto in 2011. In the back row, standing, is Leora's husband, Rafi (left), and Felix's son Ami (right). Seated in front (left to right): Naomi's husband, Michael; Felix and his great-grandson, Jackson; and Esther's son Toby.

1   Felix and Regina at their granddaughter Leora's wedding, Toronto, June 13, 2010.
2   The Opatowski family at Leora's wedding. Left to right: Ami Opatowski; Jodi
    Berkel; Toby Berkel; Miriam Opatowski; Jackson Berkel; Esther Kaufman-
    Opatowski; Leora and Rafi Wanounou; Naomi Rapponi; Michael Rapponi;
    Regina Opatowski; Felix Opatowski; Susan Opatowski; Brooke Opatowski; Fern
    Opatowski; and Nathan Opatowski.

Index

Allied forces, 111–112

American army, 109, 110–111, 113, 117–118, 120–127

American Jewish Congress, 133–134

Artman, Jakob, 40–41, 42–44, 47–48, 49, 52, 55, 57, 80–81, 97, 100–109, 114–120, 125–27, 129, 138–139

Auschwitz, xx, 2, 35, 37–100, 107–108, 122, 133–135, 140. *See also* Birkenau (Auschwitz II); Buna–Monowitz (Auschwitz III); Buna-Werke; crematoria; Czech Family Camp; D camp; Gypsy camp; Kanada; "Neutral Zone" (Auschwitz); penal barracks; quarantine camp.

Auschwitz-Birkenau. *See* Auschwitz; Birkenau (Auschwitz II).

Austria, 4, 18, 134

Baluty (Lodz), xvii, 15–17, 18. *See also* Lodz ghetto.

"the Baron." *See* Coward, Charles.

Belgian Jews, 86

Berkel, Presley (great-granddaughter), 139

Berkel, Jackson (great-grandson), 139

Berkel, Toby (grandchild), 139

Berkel-Rapponi, Naomi (granddaughter), 139

Berlin (Germany), 89, 90, 96, 122

Betar, 9–10, 144. *See also* Jabotinsky, Ze'ev; Zionism.

Bialystok (Poland), 12

Bindermichl (Austria), 125–127

Birkenau (Auschwitz II), xx, 38–42, 44–46, 55, 76, 78, 84, 85–89, 90, 99–100, 140

Blockstube, 53

Bratislava (Czechoslovakia), 102

Bricha, 122

British army, 80, 111. *See also* Allied forces.

British government, 136

British Mandate Palestine, 9–10, 122

British P O W s, 77–78, 135

Britzman, Deborah, xvi

Buna-Monowitz (Auschwitz III), 47, 76–80, 82–84, 86, 90–91, 92

Buna-Werke, 87

Cambodia, 141

Canada, 1, 131

Charnetski (Commander of Weisser Adler), xix, 26

Council of Elders. See Judenrat.

Count of Auschwitz. See Coward, Charles.

Coward, Charles ("Count of Auschwitz"), 2, 77–81, 93, 133, 135–137

crematoria, 41, 63–66, 84, 85–89, 93–97, 100, 114–115

Cyrankiewicz, Józef, 45

Czech Family Camp, 46–47, 74. See also Auschwitz; Birkenau (Auschwitz II).

Czech Jews, 46

Czechoslovakia, 18, 102

D camp, 42, 46, 89, 96, 100. See also Birkenau.

DP camp. See Displaced Persons (DP) camp.

Dachau concentration camp (Germany), 51, 62, 93, 100

Danube River, 109

death march, 99–103

Displaced Persons (DP) camp, 125, 128, 131

Ebensee (Austria), xiv, 109–20, 128, 129–131

Ekhardt, Josef, 63–65, 66, 133–135

Eichmann, Adolf, xvi–xvii, 2, 34

Emmerich (SS guard), 67

England. See British army; British government. See also Allied forces.

Felman, Shoshana, xvi

Florida (United States), 138

Frank, Hans, xix

French Jews, 77, 86

Freud, Sigmund, 27

Freund, Florian, xiv

Funny Girl (film), 68

gas chambers, 38, 40, 43, 45, 46, 47, 63–64, 65, 82. See also Auschwitz; Birkenau (Auschwitz II); crematoria.

German army, xix, 4, 23, 51, 77, 87, 93, 96, 102, 113, 117

German Communist Party, 93

German Jews, 18

German occupation of Poland, 11–12, 13

German People's Army. See German army.

Germany, 3–4, 5, 10, 11–12, 13, 18, 19, 27, 110. See also German army; Nazis.

Gestapo, 49,89. See also German army; Nazis; SS.

Gmunden (Austria), 110, 120–123, 126, 131, 138, 139

Gnat family (Regina's parents), 1, 12, 131

grandfather (maternal), 5–6

grandfather (paternal), 3, 4, 6

grandmother (maternal), 5–6

grandmother (paternal), 5

Great Britain. *See* British army; British government.

Gypsies (Roma and Sinti), 35, 39

Gypsy camp, 46, 86, 88. *See also* Birkenau (Auschwitz II).

Halifax (Canada), 131

Hallein DP camp (Austria), 131

Heydrich, Reinhard, 34

Himmler, Heinrich, 89

Hitler, Adolf, 10–11

Horowitz, Sara, xvii

Höss, Rudolf, 66

Hungarian Jews, 62–63, 64, 68–72, 75

I. G. Farben, 87, 138. *See also* Buna-Monowitz (Auschwitz III); Buna-Werke.

International Refugee Organization, 131

Israel. *See* British Mandate Palestine.

Italian Jews, 77

Italian prisoners of war (P O W s), 110

Jabotinsky, Ze'ev, 9–10. *See also* Betar; Zionism.

Jewish Committee, 121

Jewish Council. *See* Judenrat.

Jewish ghetto police, 18, 22–23. *See also* Judenrat; Lodz ghetto.

Jewish gymnasium (Lodz), 8–9

Jolinarsky (childhood friend), 10, 21–23

Judenrat, xix, 18–19, 151–152, 157. *See also* Rumkowski, Chaim.

Kanada (Auschwitz), 67–68, 97, 100

Kanada *Kommando*, 80, 83–84

kapos, 44–45, 47, 50, 54–55, 57, 59–60, 70, 106–107, 111. *See also* Manfred (kapo at Birkenau); Ziggy (kapo at Birkenau).

Kaufman, Esther (Berkel) (née Opatowski) (daughter), 1, 131, 139

Kitt, Bruno, 138

Klaus, Dr. (at Melk camp), 108

Kristallnacht, xx, 10, 19, 93

Krull, Nathan (Felix's uncle), 4

Krull, Sarah (née Opatowski, Felix's aunt), 4–5, 140

labour camp guards, 29–30, 32

Lambach (Austria), 110

Łask (Poland), 3, 4, 6

Laub, Dori, xvi

Lebensraum, xviii

Lemke (kapo in Birkenau), 96

Levi, Primo, xiv, xivn1, 78

Linz (Austria), 106, 109–110, 112, 120, 125–127

Lodz (Poland), xvii, 3, 5, 8, 13, 86, 121

Lodz ghetto, xviii–xix, 15–24, 26, 34, 140

London (England), 134, 135–136, 137

Manfred (kapo at Birkenau), 61–62, 64, 68, 71–74, 76, 79, 82, 86, 94. *See also* kapos.

Mann, Franceska, 66–68

Mauthausen concentration camp (Austria), 93, 100, 103–106, 110, 112

Max (father's friend), 4, 5, 11–12, 17–18

Mein Kampf, 10. *See also* Hitler, Adolf.

Melk concentration camp (Austria), 106–109, 110, 112

Mengele, Josef, 42–43, 86, 114, 138

Mexiko camp (Auschwitz), 75. *See also* Auschwitz.

Mischling, 51

Moishe (friend from Ebensee), 114–115, 128–130. *See also* Yankel (friend from Ebensee).

Moll, Otto (SS Colonel), 66

Monowitz (Poland), 77, 87

Montreal (Canada), 138

Mosquito *Kommando,* 79, 137–138

Munich (Germany), 147

Muselmann, 29

Nazis, xviii–xix, 14, 19, 27, 29, 51–52, 55, 60, 62, 66, 89, 134. *See also* German army; Germany; Gestapo; Hitler, Adolf; SS.

"Neutral Zone" (Auschwitz), 61–62, 69, 75

Nuremberg Trials, 137

Opatowski, Ami (son), 139

Opatowski, Brooke (granddaughter), 139

Opatowski, Esther (mother), 3, 5, 7, 9, 12, 14–17, 19, 21, 23

Opatowski, Felix: arrival at Auschwitz, 37–43; childhood in Lodz, xvii, 3–15; at D camp, 42, 53–75; on the death march, 99–103; in Gmunden, 120–131; in Ebensee, 110–120; immigration to Canada, xv, xvi, 131; interrogation at Auschwitz, 89–97;

at labour camps, 25–35; in Lodz ghetto, 15–24; at Mauthausen, 103–106; at Melk, 106–109; in quarantine camp, 40–53; working for Underground, 76–88

Opatowski, Fern (granddaughter), 139

Opatowski, Miriam (daughter), 139

Opatowski, Nathan (father), 3–5, 7–8, 10, 11–12, 15–16, 17–18, 20–22, 24, 140

Opatowski, Nathan (son), 139

Opatowski, Regina (née Gnat), 1, 121, 122, 128, 130–131, 139

Opatowski, Romek (brother), 3, 19, 20–21, 23, 140

Oświęcim (Poland), 35, 97. *See also* Auschwitz.

Ottawa (Canada), 136

Palestine. *See* British Mandate Palestine; Israel.

penal barracks (Auschwitz), 75–76

penal colony. *See* penal barracks (Auschwitz).

Phillipe (kapo in Birkenau), 96

Poland, xvii–xviii, 3–4, 5–6, 8, 11–12, 13, 32, 33, 34, 45, 87, 101, 121–122, 128, 140

Polish Jews, 11–12, 14, 18, 19, 71, 114, 128

Polish Home Army, 67, 73, 78, 86–87, 88. *See also* Polish Underground (Auschwitz).

Polish Underground (Auschwitz), 67, 73–89, 92–94, 95, 97, 122, 133. *See also* Polish Home Army.

Portugal, 4, 5

Post Exchange (PX), 122–123

POWs, 77, 78. *See* British POWs.

Poznań (Poland), 23, 25, 26, 41, 140

Primo (engineer at Buna), 76, 78–79, 137–138

quarantine camp, 40–45. *See also* Auschwitz; Birkenau (Auschwitz II).

Rapponi, Chloë (great-granddaughter), 139

Rawicz (Poland), 25

Red Cross, 77, 102, 118

Reichstag, 62

Rex (Felix's dog), xx, 6–7, 15–16, 19

Righteous Gentiles, 77, 137

Roma. *See* Gypsies (Roma and Sinti).

Rumkowski, Mordechai Chaim, 18–19

Russia. *See* Soviet Union.

Salzburg (Austria), 106, 110, 120, 131

Salzkammergut (Austria), 110

Schillinger, Josef (SS guard), 66–67

Schindler, Oskar, 77

Schreibstube, 53, 64, 90

Siberia, 128

Sigmund (German prisoner in quarantine camp), 47–53

Sinti. *See* Gypsies (Roma and Sinti).

Sola River (Oświęcim), 97

Sonderkommando, 63, 65, 66, 84–90, 95–97

"Song of the Partisans," 95–96

Soviet army, 51, 64, 87, 96, 99, 109, 111, 112

Soviet Union, 11–12, 23, 27, 128

Soviet prisoners of war (POWs), 47, 110

Spain, 4, 5

Spanish Civil War, 93

Streisand, Barbara, 68

SS (Schutzstaffel), 39, 42, 55, 64, 65, 67, 75, 80, 87, 88–91, 95, 97, 99–100, 101, 104, 107, 108–109, 112–113, 117, 133. *See also* German army; Gestapo; Nazis.

SS Lazarus, 138

SS *St. Louis*, 59, 93

Stalin, Joseph, 1

Stalingrad, 77

Star of David, 14, 39

swastika, 13

Telefunken, 11–12

Thereisenstadt, 46, 147

Third Reich. *See* Germany; Nazis.

Tolstoy, Leo, 11

Toronto (Canada), 131, 133, 135–136, 138

Underground. *See* Polish Underground (Auschwitz).

Union factory, 84

United Kingdom. *See* British army; British government.

United Nations Relief and Rehabilitation Administration (UNRRA), 128

United States, 133. *See also* Allied forces; American army.

USSR. *See* Soviet Union.

Vienna (Austria), 109, 112, 127, 134

Vilnius ghetto, 96

Vistula River (Poland), 28, 97
Vlad (member of Polish
    Underground), 92–94
Volksdeutsche, xviii–xix, 13, 14–15,
    26, 28
Wallenberg, Raoul, 77
Wanounou, Leora (grandchild), 139
Warsaw Ghetto Uprising, 73
Warsaw (Poland), xviii, 13, 66–67, 73
Weisser Adler labour camp, 25–31,
    34
Wels (Austria), 110
Wiesel, Elie, xvi, 2, 76
Yad Vashem, 77, 137
Yankel (friend from Ebensee),
    114–115, 128–129
Yellow Star. *See* Star of David.
Yugoslavia, 135, 141
Ziggy (kapo at Birkenau), 57, 59–60,
    76, 78, 80, 82–83, 89–90, 93–94.
    See also kapos.
Zionism, 9–10, 11, 139. *See also*
    Betar; British Mandate
    Palestine.
Zionist Revisionist Movement, 10.
    See also Jabotinsky, Ze'ev.

The Azrieli Foundation was established in 1989 to realize and extend the philanthropic vision of David J. Azrieli, C.M., C.Q., M.Arch. The Foundation's mission is to support a wide spectrum of initiatives in education and research. The Azrieli Foundation is an active supporter of programs in the fields of Jewish education, the education of architects, scientific and medical research, and education in the arts. The Azrieli Foundation's many well-known initiatives include: the Holocaust Survivor Memoirs Program, which collects, preserves, publishes and distributes the written memoirs of survivors in Canada; the Azrieli Institute for Educational Empowerment, an innovative program successfully working to keep at-risk youth in school; and the Azrieli Fellows Program, which promotes academic excellence and leadership on the graduate level at Israeli universities.